D1379511

LOST WORDS

LOST WORDS

A FEAST OF FORGOTTEN WORDS, THEIR ORIGINS AND THEIR MEANINGS

PHILIP HOWARD

The Robson Press

First published in Great Britain in 2012 by
The Robson Press (an imprint of Biteback Publishing Ltd)
Westminster Tower
3 Albert Embankment
London SE1 7SP

ISBN 978-1-84954-373-6

10 9 8 7 6 5 4 3 2 1

A CIP catalogue record for this book is available from the British Library.

Set in Sabon and Bodoni

Printed and bound in Great Britain by
CPI Group (UK) Ltd, Croydon CR0 4YY

CONTENTS

INTRODUCTION

Some words are born lost: 'floccinaucinihilipilifica-tion', for OOOOONE (big one). Some achieve loss: 'vambrace' from armoury, and 'topgallant' and 'mizzen-mast' (think Nelson's navy). And some have loss thrust upon them: 'Doodlebug' was the jocular euphemism for the first German flying bombs in the 1939–45 war. By giving droning death a silly name, the victims hoped to disarm its terror. But Doodlebugs have been replaced in the vocabulary by nastier terrors from the sky.

It is a guess universally acknowledged that English has the largest word-list in the world. This is because it is the mongrel language, composed not just from Latin and Teutonic, but also languages from all the countries that were once coloured pink on the atlas, and some of those that weren't, from the Round Earth's imagin'd corners. 'Jungle' and 'bungalow' came into our 'Mother Tongue' from Hindi; 'sauna' from Finnish; 'kimono' and 'bonsai' (bowl or tray cultivation) from Japanese.

So we dispute how many words there are in English. It depends on what you count as a word. Each word is surrounded by a penumbra of inflected forms, cognates, relations, separate senses and compounds. Dog is a word. But are dogs and dogged separate 'words'? Is 'dog tired' two words or one? Is 'saccharomyces cererisiae' – the formal name for bread yeast – one word, two words, or a pain in the word-box (though it shows that Latin is still the base for about three-quarters of the English vocabulary)? The word 'set' in the Oxford English Dictionary is given forty-seven separate senses and more than 60,000 words of definition.

Take in regional variations, slang, dialects, names, eponyms, toponyms, acronyms (abbreviations that can be pronounced, like Nato) and initialisms (that do not make pronounceable words, like GB), and polysyllabic medical compounds (syncytiotroph-oblontic, holoprosencephaly), and some say that English has a vocabulary of a million words.

On one count, this must be an underestimate. There is a word for each number. And since numbers are infinite (on some counts), the words for naming them must also be infinite. Local dialect and slang is as uncountable as the laughter of the waves of the sea. The humble woodlouse has many local names in Britain: higgy-hog, cheeselog, pill bug, chiggy pig, rolypoly and lice unrecorded on paper ... Each generation and group of children invent private jargons and slang to keep out adults.

At least we can count the number of words in a particular person's vocabulary.

Semantic psychologists assert that an American sixteen-year-old has on average a vocab of 10,000–12,000 words; and that a graduate has between 20,000 and 25,000. Look at such averages through narrowed eyes.

We should distinguish between active and passive vocabulary. Active are the words we actually use. Passive are potential words that lie dormant in our semantic lockers, such as '-gate', the much overused suffix from Watergate, and '-phobia', as in 'Europhobia', which can mean hatred either of Europe or of its currency – or, in Australia, of a wallaroo, a large kangaroo. We hope that such clichés, as with 'Budgetgate', 'explore every avenue' and 'leave no stone unturned' will become laughing stocks and die of shame. But they don't.

At least we can count a particular text. Or can we? Take Shakespeare. Bean-counters have calculated that Shakespeare uses 884,647 words in 29,066 distinct forms, including proper names. But what counts as a distinct word?

We all create the language, not just Shakespeare, professors, schoolmistresses and Noam Chomsky. Language is the only true democracy. Pop songs and advertising slogans do more than Milton can to justify semantic creation to man. Children continually create their own jargon: note how 'wicked' has come to mean 'super-duper-doli-dacious' on the playground. We all remake the meanings of words to suit our contemporary purposes.

Observe the rambling career of the little adjective 'nice'. It came into English from the Latin *nescius*, ignorant, 'not-knowing'. After several metamorphoses, it came to mean something like 'precise' for males and, in the male chauvinist bias of language, 'fast, immoral, lascivious' for women. By the Victorian era it had turned into a genteel term of commendation. Now it has changed its colours again, to mean something like 'nasty'. 'You're a nice friend, I must say,' is no longer a hurrah-phrase. Au contraire. On another note, 'silly' originally meant 'holy'.

All languages are continually changing and growing, unless they are truly dead languages, such as Aztec and the runes of Old English. *Panta rhei* – eveything is in a state of flux; especially English.

In such a state, does it make sense to revive lost words? Words fade away when nobody uses them anymore. They become literally 'useless'. Is it not, therefore, a work of supererogation to try to revive 'lost' words? Are we not grave-robbers of the language, who will dig up only corpses?

Well, to an extent, Karl Popper. But some words are not dead, but merely sleeping. And some of them express a meaning more precisely than any possible synonym.

In fact, there are no exact synonyms. Gorse, furze and whin name the same prickly plant with yellow flowers into which it is a pain to fall or hit your golf ball, but they each have a long trail of individual connections, connotations and regional references. Some sleeping words are interesting, amusing and even useful.

Take, for example, 'quaresimal'. It is used to describe a meal as meagre, skimpy, austere, having the qualities of inadequate (fasting, hungry) grub. It is an adaptation of the Italian word for Lenten. James Joyce, intoxicated with the labyrinths of his verbosity, in a letter of 1923 wrote: 'Can we not have a quaresimal dinner somewhere together?' Showing off? Of course. But 'quaresimal' is a more satisfying word to get one's mouth around than Lenten or stingy.

We should speak English in a common denominator pronunciation to our fellow-speakers, as far as possible. To talk posh or Mockney is irritating. That is why we have invented Estuary Speak, as a jocular neutral pronunciation. But we should collect the largest vocabulary that we can. It is a sign of education, interest and pleasure. A wide and various word-store is a mark of a civilised human being. And 'civilised' is a word that merits inspection. Non? The following words are not lost, but dormant. Here are some more sleeping words that are worth a whistle.

ACCISMUS

Pronounce: 'Back this mouse.' An insincere and feigned refusal of something that is earnestly desired. An old term of rhetoric. Adaptation of the Ancient Greek word for coyness or affectation.

Chambers, 1753: 'Cromwell's refusal of the crown may be brought as an example of an Accismus.'

Richter's Levana, 1876: 'A woman uses no figure of eloquence – her own, at most, excepted – so often as that of accismus.'

This narrow psychological term is often appropriate to the English, out of politeness, genteelism, hypermodesty or unselfishness. It merits revival for its precision, provided by no other word.

As in: 'No, please, I really would like YOU to have the last éclair.'

ACNESTIS

That part of the back between the shoulder blade and the bum (loins) that an animal cannot reach in order to scratch. Adapted from the Greek for the spine or backbone.

The Observer, 1927: 'That spot known to crossword-solvers as the acnestis.'

I admit that opportunities to use this word will be rare outside the crossword, but it explains why your dog rolls on the ground in apparent ecstasy. And it is a critical example of onomatomania, 'word-madness', or intense mental anguish at the inability to recall some word or to name a thing. We all suffer from it.

As in: 'Dear girl: please take this scratcher – what is the damn thing called? Damn onomatomania – and apply it to my acnestis.'

AGERASIA

The quality of not growing old. The non-appearance of the signs of age. A green old age. From the Greek for eternal youth: *a-*, privative, and *geeras*, old age.

Leo H. Grindon, *Life; Its Nature, Varieties and Phenomena*, 1863: 'Agerasia belongs only to the soul: this alone lives in perpetuity of youth.'

There are many words in English that have a similar meaning to agerasia, but this is the only one that I can find that does not carry pejorative implications and connotations of immaturity and childishness. Therefore worth reviving as a hurrah pro-word.

As in: 'Your agerasia, Isabel, is a consequence of the eternally questing spirit of Thetis, and interest in others.'

AGRESTIC

Countrified. Of or pertaining to the country. Rural, rustic. Hence (unkindly) uncouth. Pronounce to rhyme with 'majestic'. From Latin *ager*, *agrum*, a field. Cf. 'domestic', and, for formation, 'forensic'.

Words were mostly coined and changed by city slickers, who took a snobbish view of their agrestic roots. This is part of the stock battle between town and country, which has been fought since Confucius, Theocritus and Horace. Horace was lyrical about the agrestic charms of his Sabine farm but his lyrics were performed in the big city.

Evelyn in *Pepys' Diary*, 1703: 'He has his time for his agrestic flute.'

Disraeli, *Endymion*, 1880: 'A delightful ramble to some spot of agrestic charm.'

As the country is increasingly buried beneath concrete and asphalt, we need to preserve the country-side in the lexicon if we cannot manage it on the ground.

As in: 'Shall we pack the picnic, Myrtle? I have agrestic urges this fine morning.'

APODICTIC

Incontrovertible. Of clear demonstration. Established on incontrovertible evidence. Rhymes with 'Slap on Pritt Stick'. From the Greek *apodeiknunai*, to show off, demonstrate, via Latin. The analogical spelling is -dict-.

Coleridge, 1816: 'In the heights of geometry there exist truths of apodictic force in reason, which the mere understanding strives in vain to comprehend.'

Right on, Samuel Comberbache, when it comes to the centre of inversion of circles. Aaargh!

Sir Thomas Urquhart, 'Ekskubalauron, or the discovery of a most exquisite jewel', 1652: 'This apodictick course to infer consequences from infallible maximes.'

This is a philosopher's word, favoured by moralists such as Kant. It is shorter and neater than incontrovertible.

As in: 'It is as apodictic as two plus two equals four that you are not suited to become a nurse, Doris.'

ASPECTABUND

Expressive in the face. Showing one's feelings as an extravert. Rhyme, approximately, with 'Your specs are found'. After the Latin *lacrimabundus*, weeping, *osculabundus*, kissing, *moribundus*, dying: *-bundus* creates a verbal adjective with an active force.

So aspectabund means exhibiting one's aspect or feelings.

J. Downes, 'Roscius Anglicus', 1708: 'On the Stage, he's very Aspectabund, wearing a Farce in his Face.'

Wearing one's feelings on one's face can be as dodgy as wearing one's heart on one's sleeve. But in general we prefer faces that are open and expressive to those that are closed and secretive.

Aspectabund describes a quality that is good for actors and pop singers, not so good for spies and bankers.

As cosmetic procedures continue to work their magic, perhaps the very notion of having an expressive face will soon be forgotten. Meanwhile, let's hear it for aspectabund.

As in: 'You do not need to wag your tail and bark at me, you aspectabund hound, Alfie. I am aware that it is your dinnertime. Here. Good boy.'

BALAAMITE

Somebody who is avariciously religious for the sake of financial gain, for example televangelists in the American South and peccant Presbies in Ulster. Rhyme, approximately, with 'Hail 'em right'.

Milton, 1648: 'God hath so dispos'd the mouth of these Balaams, that coming to Curse, they have stumbled into a kind of Blessing.'

Balaam was the prophet sent by the Warlord of Moab to parley with the Israelites in order to curse them. An angel bars his road. Donkey shies. Balaam falls, sprains his ankle and curses his poor moke. The donkey speaks back. So Balaam praises the Israelites instead of cursing them.

Later the Israelites killed him, a piece of monstrous ingratitude for which the Old Testament offers no explanation or excuse. Unfortunately, by II Peter ii:15, the anthropomokey story is revised, and Balaam is portrayed simply as a greedy bastard.

As in: 'Politicians as well as priests can be Balaamites, Tom.'

BAYARD

Somebody who has the self-confidence of ignorance. One blind to the light of knowledge.

Originally this meant a bay-coloured horse, and, specifically, the bay-coloured magic steed given by Charlemagne to Renaud, one of the four sons of Aimon, famous in medieval romance. Hence, a kind of mock-heroic allusive name for any horse; cf. the occasional use of Rosinante, Pegasus, Bucephalus.

Isaac Barrow, sermon, 1677: 'The bold and blind Bayards (who usually out of self-conceit are so exceedingly confident of their election and salvation).'

The progress from a bay-coloured horse to a conceited horse's arse is obscure, but popular proverbs and phrases converted 'bayard' to blindness or blind recklessness.

1630: 'As boldly as blind bayard rusheth into battle.'

This horsey epithet is a useful learned put-down for such tiresome prats.

As in: 'I congratulate you on your speech, Charles; you are a true bayard of debate.'

BOUFFAGE

An enjoyable or satisfying meal. Adoption of the Old French word. Rhyme, approximately, with 'You're large'.

Randle Cotgrave, in his French–English dictionary of 1611, defined it as: 'Any meat that (eaten greedily) fills the mouth and makes the cheeks to swell; cheek-puffing meat.' In other words, a blow-out.

Sir Thomas Browne, 'Letter to a Friend', 1672: 'His inwards and flesh remaining could make no bouffage, but a light bit for the grave.'

This gutsy old word may be of less use in these sad days of salad and weight-watching than it was in the merry old England of roast beef and beer and pies, but it can still come in handy when taking small boys out for a treat.

As in: 'To celebrate your victory over Sedbergh, Harry, let us have a team outing for a bouffage at Joan's Kitchen.'

CACHINNATOR

Somebody who laughs too loud and too much. Adaptation of the Latin *cachinnare*, to laugh loudly or immoderately. Compare and contrast 'agelastic' and 'hypergelast'.

Robert Chambers, *Wheesht*, 1800: 'They mark a cachinnator as a man to be avoided.'

There are fewer of these noisy pests among us than we suppose; because their parents presumably strangled them at an early age. There is no other word that fills this precise hole in the vocabulary: laugher, smiler, chortler, chuckler, shrieker? They don't quite do it, do they?

Note the cognates.

Robert Browning, *The Ring and the Book*, 1868: 'He moved to mirth and cachinnation all.'

Nathaniel Hawthorne, *Moses*, 1846: 'Which threatened death on the slightest cachinnatory indulgence.'

Laughter is a blessing. But not when it comes from a hyena. This useful lost word fills a hole in the lexicon, e.g., to describe the hysterical crowd laughter at some crude comedians.

As in: 'I agree that he is funny, but we must take care not to annoy others by becoming cachinnators. Non?'

CHARIENTISM

A rhetorical term to describe saying a disgreeable thing in an agreeable way. Adaptation of the Greek word for gracefulness of style, by way of Latin and French.

George Puttenham, Elizabethan scribbler, *The Arte of English Poesie*, 1589: 'The Greeks call it charientismus.'

Puttenham defines and illustrates figures of speech, and suggests vulgar names for Greek and Latin originals, e.g., 'single supply, ringleader, and middle-marcher' (zeugma, prozeugma and mezozeugma).

The British Apollo, 1709: 'A Charientism is that Species of an Irony, which couches a Disagreeable Sense under Agreeable Expressions.'

As in: 'You have delighted us long enough with your piano-playing, Mary.'

CHRESTOMATHIC

Devoted to the learning of useful matters. From the Greek for learning useful things, by way of French. 'Chrestomathy', the noun, means a collection of choice passages from an author or authors, especially one compiled to assist in the acquisition of a language.

Southey, *The Doctor*, 1834–37: 'Which the said Jeremy [Bentham] proposes should form part of the course of studies in his Chrestomathic school.'

But what are useful matters? For some it is how to solve simultaneous quadratic equations or how to darn a hole in a sock; for others it is how to predict the winner in the 2.30 at Ascot.

As in: 'I can see that it is fiddly fun, but is philately seriously chrestomathic?'

COLLOQUIALIST

Somebody who excels in conversation; a (good) talker. Apparently from the Latin *colloqui*, to speak with, converse. Cf. French *colloquer*. *Loquor* in Latin means 'I speak'. Rhyme, roughly, with 'No joke I missed'.

1824: 'As a colloquialist Johnson has scarcely a rival.'

1834: 'That their interviews were employed in the prosy manner suggested by the lovely colloquialist.'

This is a misunderstood lost word. From the Latin *colloquium* (conversation), it is properly employed to refer to words as they are used in a conversational sense. Cf. Harriet Beecher Stowe, *Uncle Tom's Cabin*, 1850: 'The colloquy between Tom and Eva was interrupted by a hasty call from Miss Ophelia.'

However, many are under the misapprehension that 'colloquial' means slang, coarse or sub-standard usage. So 'colloquialist' has come to mean somebody who uses slang.

1821: 'All this, as the colloquialists say, is very well for a joke.'

Making conversation is a defining characteristic of mortals, so let us try to be colloquialists.

As in: 'Let us have a good natter as cheerful colloquialists.'

DEIPNOSOPHIST

A master/mistress of the art of dining.

Taken from the title of a famous Greek work of Athenaeus of Naucratis in Egypt, *The Learned Banquet*, probably completed in about AD 200, after the death of Commodus in AD 192. It is a polyhistoric (phew!) symposium. At the 'banquet', which extends over several days, philosophy, literature, medicine, law and other interests are represented by a large number of guests, who in some cases bear historical names, and who sometimes make jokes, or attempts at jokes.

1845: 'Spanish cookery, a subject which is well worth the inquiry of any antiquarian deipnosophist'.

There is a hole in the language between, on the one place, a gourmand and, on the other, a gourmet with a taste for entertaining and illuminating chatter as well as caviar. A witty society called the Deipnosophists dines regularly at the Athenaeum.

As in: 'Stop chomping, James, and entertain us as a true deipnosophist.'

DESIDERIUM

An ardent desire or wish; longing or wish, properly for a thing you once possessed and now miss; a sense of loss. A material sister to the geographical nostalgia. The Latin word means longing, sense of want; from *desiderare*, which we have rendered into stiff-collared English as 'desiderate'. Rhyme, roughly, with 'Daisy, Mary, Tom'.

Swift, letter to Pope, 1715: 'When I leave a country I think as seldom as I can of what I loved or esteemed in it, to avoid the desiderium which of all things makes life most uneasy.'

Gilbert White, *The Natural History and Antiquities of Selborne*, 1789: 'This strange affection probably was occasioned by that desiderium.'

This is a strong word. It is appropriate for regret for lost youth or innocence, for the great love of your life or for the Utopian community to which you once belonged, which was destroyed by the forces of evil. It is not the word for your lost specs or having missed the bus. Desiderium for lost opportunities is part of growing up.

As in: 'Sam, I have a desiderium for golden days of playing fields and jolly boating weather.'

DULCARNON

A person in a dilemma; somebody 'halting between two opinions'. Rhyme, approximately, with 'Pull, Ma! Non'. This is a Medieval Latin corruption of the Arabic word for two-horned, *bicornis*, *cornutus*; literally, 'the possessor of two horns'.

Richard Stanyhurst, 'A Treatise Contayning a Playne and Perfect Description of Irelande', in Holinshed, 1577: 'S. Patrike considering that these silly souls (as all dulcarnons for the most partare) more to be terrified from infidelitie through the paines of Hell, than allured to Christiantie by the joys of Heaven.'

Originally dulcarnon meant a dilemma, before it came to mean somebody *in* a dilemma.

Some say that dulcarnon was also a medieval appellation of the Pythagorean theorem, Euclid I, 47 (it is supposed from its somewhat two-horned figure).

A useful word to use when choosing between a Twix and a Mars Bar for Molly – and imagine Stanyhurst rolling over in his grave.

As in: 'I am in a perfect dulcarnon of whether to play Mozart or Berlioz: Mozart wins.'

EMBRANGLE

To entangle. To confuse or perplex. This is a phonetic variation of the French *branler*, to shake. Whereof the ultimate origin is uncertain. Its meaning is influenced by wrangle (fourteenth century), and possibly by brabble and brawl, with which it is nearly synonymous.

Coleridge, letter, 1811: 'The perplexities with which I have been thorned and embrangled.'

We should not give the kiss of life to words merely for their sound – the Swinburnian fallacy. (What sort of 'should' is that, Philip?) But embrangle does sound more thorny and inextricable than its near synonyms.

As in: 'I am embrangled in tomorrow's simultaneous quadratic equations for homework, Lewis.'

FATIDICAL

Prophetic. Gifted with the power of prophecy. Adaptation of the Latin *fatum* (fate) plus *dic-*, the weak root of Latin *dicere*, to speak.

You might question whether we need yet another word for this activity when we already have a lexicon of prudent, predictive, prophetic, Lobby correspondents, weather-forecasting and other forms of spurious fortune-telling. But pretending to foresee the future is still a popular superstition. And fatidical has a peculiar resonance for inanimate and unintentional forecasting.

So Carlyle (who else?), 1829: 'The fatidical fury spreads wider and wider.'

James Howell (Charles II's Historiographer Royal), 1645: 'The Ancients write of some Trees, that they are Fatidical.'

As in: 'Much as I respect your fatidical powers, Adam, I prefer not to risk my shirt on this race.'

FINIFUGAL

Of or pertaining to shunning the end (of anything). A kind of deliberate dawdling and dilatoriness. From Latin *finis*, end, plus *fuga*, flight. Rhymes, approximately, with 'Mini-bugle'.

L. A. Tollemache, *Journal of Education*, September 1883: 'In modern as well as in ancient times, the finifugal tendency is apparent.'

Many things are worth being finifugal with: the Iliad or any other good book; a good meal; prime time with one's children and friends; walking Alfie and other yappers in the park. No other word in the huge lexicon of English so satisfactorily describes the pleasures of virtuous procrastination.

The converse is finiprecipitous, hastening the end: as with a visit to the dentist, eating slimy suet pudding or filling in forms for Mr Taxman. I do not know whether the latter word exists, but it does now. So there.

As in: 'Don't be finifugal, Charlie: eat up your delicious carrots and we can go and play footy on the common.'

FLESHMENT

The action of 'fleshing', hence the excitement result-
ing from a first success.

Eh? This comes, like much English, from the
jargon of hawking and hunting. To 'flesh' means to
reward (a hawk or hound) with a portion of the
flesh of the game killed, to excite his eagerness in the
chase. Hence in a wider sense, to render (an animal)
eager for prey by the taste of blood.

Shakespeare, *King Lear*, 1605: 'And in the fleshment of this dead exploit [he] Drew on me here again.'

Excitement that results from witnessing a first
success can be a great pleasure; for example, when a
child declines 'mensa' or rides a bicycle unaided for
the first time. What an ugly word for such a delightful concept.

But do not be carried away by fleshment. Just
because you win a small amount on the horses, do
not let fleshment fool you that the wide world is
your oyster.

As in: 'I experience great fleshment when we read
Hamlet together, Hermione.'

FOIBLESSE

A characteristic weakness; a failing. Hence, a liking or 'weakness' for something. Adaptation of the Old French obsolete spelling for *faiblesse*, *faible*: feeble. Rhyme with 'Boy, Bless!'

'Foible' is a boo-word. It reeks of bad habits, wrong turnings, and decisions of dubious merit. 'Foiblesse' makes the notion of having a weakness for something seem OK, acceptable, even commendable.

T. H. Croker, in his introduction to his version of *Orlando Furioso*, 1755: 'I must acknowledge my own foiblesse in conception of a sensible pleasure.'

Francis Jeffrey, literary critic and editor, in the *Edinburgh Review*, 1813: 'Our own foiblesse for such speculations might tempt us to select a few more examples.'

Contrast and compare 'hamartia', the flaw that precipitates the destruction of a tragic hero.

Foiblesse is not an unconscious sin but a conscious bias or liking. Nothing to be ashamed of. But un petit peu pretentious, non? Still, a pretty, lost word worth revival.

As in: 'Circulate the port, dear boy – you know my foiblesse.'

FOMES

Stuff that can infect you with disease. Any object that may transmit a communicable disease to another user. Rhyme with 'No knees'. Plural 'fomites'; rhyme with 'Snow Whites'. Adaptation of the Latin for 'touchwood, tinder'. 'Any porous substance capable of absorbing and retaining contagious effluvia.'

Gentleman's Magazine, 1773: 'If this putrid ferment could be more immediately corrected, a stop would probably be put to the flux, and the fomes of the disease likewise removed.'

Figuratively, Thomas Ken (1637–1711), chaplain to Charles II, *Hymnotheo*, 1711: 'Concupiscential Fomes, which possess'd / The Parents thus, was on their Race impress'd.'

If you wear rubber gloves to shake hands and balance precariously in the Tube rather than touch the same handholds as the disease-ridden public, or are a contortionist who opens bathroom doors with an elbow in terror of infection, this is the forgotten word for you.

As in: 'The chapter on the fall of the euro you may omit, Cecily. It is too sensational and a fomes for euroscepticism.'

FUBSY

Words die because nobody uses them. This does not always mean that they are useless.

Fubsy means (of the figure, limbs etc.) fat and squat. As a noun, a fubsy is (was) a small, chubby person. Perhaps it comes from a blending of 'fat' and 'chubby' (presumably from the rotundity of the chub fish).

Madame D'Arblay, diary, April 1970: 'Her daughter, a fubsy, good-humoured, merry old maid.'

George Sala, 1879: 'She was a squat, fubsy little old woman.'

Odd how the epithet gets applied to women, not men, eh?

Nothing works as economically and poetically as fubsy. Here is a dying word that deserves resurrection.

As in: 'The man on the Tube was fubsy and wouldn't budge.'

FUGLEMAN

A right marker. A soldier especially expert and well drilled, formally placed in front of a regiment or company as an example or model to the others in their exercises. Adaptation of the German *flügel*, wing, plus *mann*, man. The leader of the file.

William Taylor in the *Monthly Review* LXXIV, 1814: 'Like the fugleman of a regiment, he overacts the movements which he would excite in others.'

Brits find the first L in 'f(l)ugleman' tricky to pronounce, and have dropped it. We still use the word literally, when the Sergeant Major bellows: 'Right Maaarkers!' and the fuglemen in the Black Watch or other less well-drilled regiments stamp to attention and march out for the companies to form up on.

A useful word for a leader who compels the members of his organisation to dance to his tune.

As in: 'Oh, please act as fugleman, Duncan, and demonstrate the Strathspey steps of the Foursome.'

FULSOME

This ancient word (first recorded 1250) is not lost but morphing. 'Fulsome praise' is now widely and misleadingly used as a compliment: 'Great praise.' But in its journey down the centuries fulsome has come to mean excessive, over-the-top, cloying through surfeit.

For example, the praise given by an excitable British sports commentator to the performance of the British runner who has just come last in the first heat of his event in the Olympic Games; or the school report of a child whose parents are potential contributors to the school athletics or dramatic fund. We do not speak of fulsome abuse or fulsome criticism. Now chiefly used to describe excessive flattery or the like.

Richard Bentley, Boyle Lecture, 1692: 'They were puffed up with the fulsome Flatteries of their Philosophers and Sophists.'

Use only if you are confident that you are being critical, not complimentary.

As in: 'I enjoyed our game of footy, Jeremy; but your description of me as the Rooney of the backyard might be deemed, by a purist, as fulsome.'

GARBIST

One who is skilled in polite behaviour; an expert in good manners and 'etiket'. This comes directly from *garbe*, the French word for grace and elegance, ultimately from the Old High German for preparation and adornment.

1640: 'Yes, this is backsword Complement: this wipes off the false praise which the first thrust on: you must bee seene in both, or you are no true garbist else.'

The golden rule of good manners for the garbist is to think of others before himself or herself. In other words, garbism is self-effacing unselfishness: to put others first, and not to ask for any reward.

As in: 'Be a garbist, Katy: do not gabble while you gobble with your mouth full.'

GAUM

To stare vacantly and vapidly. Pronounce to rhyme with 'warm'.

Do not confuse it with other 'gaums', meaning: to handle, especially in some improper fashion (Swift: 'Don't be mauming and gauming a Body so. Can't you keep your filthy Hands to yourself?'); to smear with a sticky substance; to daub (something sticky) on the surface; attention, notice, heed (variant of 'gome').

Gauming is easily identified as the behaviour of simpletons and open-mouthed gapers the world over. So do not confuse gaum with 'gaum-like', defined by the big dictionary as 'Having an intelligent look'.

For 'gaum' the gaper, 'Cumberland & Westmoreland Dialect', 1839: 'A body knaas better haw tae carry thersel when they er amang gentlefowk: yan leaks nit quite sae gaumin.'

Compare and contrast with 'gove', defined as 'to stare stupidly'; except for *Webster's Third New International*, which defines 'gove' as to stare idly.

As in: 'Stop gauming, Holly, and give me a hand with the washing-up.'

GOBEMOUCHE

A simple silly sucker. One who accepts all news, however improbable or absurd. Rhyme, approximately, with 'Bob louche?' Adaptation of the French *gobe-mouches* (from *gober*, to swallow, plus *mouche*, a fly) flycatcher (bird and plant), credulous person.

In French *gobemouches* is singular and plural, though Littré points out that gobe-mouche might be written on the analogy of chasse-mouche. English writers treat the French form as a plural and use gobemouche for the singular.

A Handbook for Travellers in Spain, 1845: 'Their idle stories are often believed by the gobemouche class of book-making travellers.'

In our age of credulity, why not reintroduce such a vivid metaphor?

As in: 'There was an old lady who swallowed a fly. Don't ask me why. She was a gobemouche.'

GONGOOZLER

Someone who stares protractedly at nothing, into thin air. First recorded in writing in 1904. Rhyme, approximately, with 'Long foozler'.

The word was originally applied, reputedly in the dialect of the Lake District, specifically to someone who stares at activity on a canal. Its origins are obscure but its elements may have a connection with the Lincolnshire word 'gawn' (to stare vacantly or curiously), and 'gooze' (to gape).

The New Yorker, 1986: 'I stopped off in the Galeana Sports-park to watch a game on one of three huge outdoor screens that the city had provided for gongoozlers like me.'

In our age of constant television there is renewed room for a word for a vacant couch potato. There should always be small space in life to stand and stare at the remarkable activities of the fellow travellers on our Ship of Fools. No space for staring into vacancy. But it is better to get out and do something rather than watch others. Life is doing as well as watching.

As in: 'Come on, Henry; get your pads on! Stop being a gongoozler.'

GOUND

The gunk that collects in the corner of the eye. Foul matter, especially that secreted in the eye. Pronounce to rhyme with 'pound'. Derived from Gothic and Old English *gund*, matter (pus?).

John Lydgate (c. 1370–1451), the English poet and monk, *Pilgrimage of the Life of Man*, 1426: 'Cleaneth away [from the eye] all ordure, / The gound, and everything unpure.'

And while we are gunking, take in 'illutible': stuff that cannot be washed away. Rhyme, approximately, with 'Is suitable'. Latin *il-* is the assimilated form of the negative prefix 'l', as in 'il-legal' and 'il-literate'. 'Illutible' fits a wide range of subjects, from bicycle grease to adultery.

And in the cognate dirty water, please note 'abluvion': substances or things that are washed away. You have probably never stared at the dirty water washing down the drain and wondered, 'Is there a word for that?' Now you will be for ever blessed (cursed?) with the knowledge that there is indeed one

As in: 'Allow me to use my red spotted hanky to remove the gound from your eye, Ella: it is not illutible but abluvion.'

GOVE

To stare stupidly. Of obscure (northern) origin. A suggested connection with 'gaw', of similar meaning, cannot be traced.

James Hogg, the 'Ettrick Shepherd', *The Queen's Wake*, 1813 (which made Hogg's reputation as a poet): 'The wild beasts of the forest came / And goved around, charmed and amazed.'

The *OED* and all other big dictionaries define gove as to stare stupidly. Except for *Webster's Third International*, which defines it as 'to stare idly'. We can be confident that the fact that *Webster's Third* was edited by a chap called Gove has nothing to do with this lexicographical decision, can't we?

As in: 'Stop goving at me like a loony, boy, and construe.'

GRAMAUNGERE

A great or delicious meal. A blow-out. Rhyme, (very) roughly, with 'black horse hair'. Adaptation of the Old French *grant mangier*, a great meal.

The *Oxford English Dictionary* notes: 'Not from the original French, which has "Do you think you can eat up all the pagans by yourselves?"' Eh?

Sounds good, but I could read more of that. English is rich in gluttonous words: tuck, Bacchanalia, beano, Rowlands, bunfight, fleshpots, browsing and sluicing ... but there is always room for another gutsy word in these hard times of virtual gluttony.

As in: 'To celebrate your First XV cap, John, I propose to take you to Joan's Kitchen for a gramaungere to satisfy even Billy Bunter.'

GRIMGRIBBER

Legal or other technical jargon; learned gibberish.

The toponym of an imaginary estate, extemporised in a discussion between two sham Counsels respecting a marriage settlement. Source: Sir Richard (*The Spectator*) Steele, *The Conscious Lovers* (derived from Terence's *Andria*), 1723: Mrs Seal: 'The single Question is, whether the Intail is such, that my Cousin Sir Geoffry is necessary in this Affair?' Bram: 'Yes, as to the Lordship of Tretriplet, but not as to the Messuage of Grimgribber.'

The success of this comedy was in part due to the acrimonious reactions provoked by the reviews of it in Steele's periodical, *The Theatre*. Thereafter grimgribber became a synonym for learned rubbish.

Our age is rich in high-sounding gibberish. But are we helping to clean the language by adding to the cartloads of metaphors for the crap cant?

As in: 'Cracking speech, William: it was a fine specimen of grimgribber.'

GRISEOUS

Rather grey. Greyish. Scientifically and specifically in zoology and botany, bluish grey, pearl grey. Rhyme, approximately, with 'busy fuss' or 'size a mouse'. Both pronunciations are recorded. From the Old French adaptation of the medieval Latin *griseus*.

1828, zoologically: 'Tail-feathers wedge-shaped, griseous, spotted with black.'

Here is an aberrant use from a dictionary of entomology, which should know better, 1826: 'Griseous (griseus), white mottled with black or brown.'

This rare word is problematic and liable to confusion both in denotation and pronunciation.

Transferred, *Contemporary Review*, 1893: 'French soil and notably French skies are griseous.'

How much more griseous are English skies.

We need to revive a word that means 'sort of grey', 'a sable silvered', like the beard of Hamlet senior. It is a kinder word than grey, or white, to describe the hair of the elderly.

As in: 'Don't bother to get up yet, Olivia. The morning looks distinctly griseous.'

HAMARTIA

The fault or error that entails the destruction of the tragic hero (with particular reference to the *Poetics* of Aristotle). In Greek, *hamartia* means fault, failure, guilt.

Aristotle defined the Athenian art of tragedy. It should have hamartia (tragic error); peripeteia (complication); catastrophe (world turned upside down); anagnorisis (recognition of disaster); and catharsis (purgation of the audience through pity and terror for the poor bleeding [often literally] sod on the stage).

D. W. Lucas, *Aristotle Poetics*, 1968: 'The essence of hamartia is ignorance combined with the absence of wicked intent.'

This is a serious pre-Christian word, not to be uttered inadvisedly, lightly or wantonly, to describe some peccadillo such as failure to get up on time – tiresome though such weaknesses may be.

As in: 'Your indifference to the effect that your sarcasm has on others approaches a tragic hamartia, Christopher.'

HOOVERISE

To be economical, sparing or stingy, especially in the use of food. The eponym of Herbert C. Hoover (1874–1964), Food Commissioner 1917–19, and President of the United States 1929–33.

Poor old Herbie. The thirty-first President not only presided over his country's descent into the Great Depression, but he also gave his name to two pejorative words, hooverise and Hooverville, a temporary shantytown. As US Food Commissioner he was accused by the hungry of being unduly stingy with food rationing. Later, fairly or not, he became identified with the failure of government relief programmes during the Great Depression.

1932: 'Once before he made us Hooverise when Wilson had his war.'

1973: 'It was all like some weird Hooverville. They were cooking their suppers over open fires.'

Smart historical words for inelegant acts and states.

As in: 'I am sorry. We have to hooverise, so it's old clothes and porridge, AGAIN.'

ILLWILLY

Cherishing ill-will. Malevolent, malignant, ill-disposed. Do not confuse this with evil-willy if you are going in for resurrecting dead words. Evil-willy describes the possession of desires that are evil; illwilly infers that the possessor cherishes and enjoys his malignancy.

Scottish proverb, 1721: 'An illwilly cow should have short horns.'

There is a gap in contemporary English for an epithet to describe somebody, such as a leader of the BNP, who is not merely nasty but revels in his nastiness. It is, however, not easy to take any word seriously that ends in 'willy'.

As in: 'You are illwilly, Timothy, to enjoy teasing your sister.'

INCOMPETIBLE

Not within one's competence or capacity. Not compatible. Not properly applicable or suitable to. Inappropriate. Rhymes (roughly) with 'In your convertible'.

Do not confuse this with 'incompatible'. Incompatible describes the wrong tool for the job. IncomPETible describes the wrong person for doing it. Latin *competere* means to be suitable or fit, as in competent.

Gilbert Burnet (enthusiastic Glaswegian preacher), *The Earth*, 1684: 'The characters of the New Jerusalem are very hard to be understood: some of them being incompetible to a terrestrial state, and some of them to a celestial.'

We surely need a single word to describe us as being not fit for purpose, which is part of the human condition most of the time.

As in: 'You had better drive, Suzanne. I feel more than usually incompetible today.'

INDREAD

To dread inwardly. To feel an inward or secret dread. Rhyme with 'sinned red'. From the Old English *ondraedan*. Cf. 'adread', Old English *ofdraeden*, to make afraid, terrify.

Thomas Hudson's translation of Du Bartas's *Judith*, 1584: 'So Isaac's sons indreading for to feel / This tyrant, who pursued them at the heel, / Dissundring [splitting up] fled.'

We all have these secret dreads that keep us awake at night from time to time, tossing and turning with worry. Knowing the name for the condition is not going to make things any better. The remedy is to keep a good book, which you are reluctant to put down and eager to take up, on the bedside table.

Cf. 'terriculament', a source or object of dread, especially of needless dread: a bugbear.

As in: 'Do not indread that you are sitting for an exam for which you have not revised adequately, Grant. This is a common indread.'

INDRI

The babacoote is a small lemurine animal of Madagascar (*Indri* or *Lichanotus brevicaudatus*), living in trees, with soft woolly hair, very long hind legs and a very short tail. I agree that this is not a word we are going to need often, except possibly as an insult. But its etymology exhibits the mad richness of English word formation.

The French naturalist Sommerat was exploring Madagascar around 1780. The name is an erroneous application of the Malagasy exclamation 'Indry!' (Look! Lo! Behold!) or 'Indry iz' (There he is!). The only name for the little creature in Malagasy is 'babakoto', literally 'father–child'.

Daily News, 1890: 'The avahi is still more nearly related to the indri, of which there is not a specimen in the zoo.'

As in: 'Stop monkeying about like an indri, Matthew!'

INQUILINATE

To live in a strange place; to be a lodger or temporary sojourner (Latin *sub diurnus*). Don't/aren't we all inquilines on our Ship of Fools? Rhyme, Oz-ly, with 'Infill me, mate!' Adaptation of the Latin *inquilinus*, an inmate of the same house, a tenant or lodger. The noun 'inquiline' is a sojourner, a lodger or indweller.

In zoology this is the technical term for an animal (or bird, or insect) that lives in the nest or abode of another.

Compton Mackenzie, *Sinister Street*, 1914: 'Half the inquilines of a night and even some of the less transient lodgers ultimately escaped owing her money.'

For the specialised zoological meaning, *The Athenaeum*, 1882: 'Numerous inquilines of other orders of insects found in ants' nests, which the ants never molest, but even take great care of.'

We can use a precise name for the inquiline enjoying a sleepover.

As in: 'May I borrow your sofa tonight, Ant? I promise to be an inquiline, not a fixture.'

INSORDESCENT

Increasing in filthiness. Grubby, grubbier, grubbiest, like the state of the pavements outside McDonald's. An adaptation of the Latin *insordescens*, the present participle of *insordescere*, to become foul or dirty. Pronounce, roughly, to rhyme with 'In poor descent'.

Samuel Chandler, translation of Philippus van Limborch's *History of the Inquisition*, 1731: 'A Man is said to be insordescent in Excommunication, who, after he hath by name been Excommunicate, persists in that Excommunication for a year ... He must be deprived of his Benefice for Insordescence.'

We have a lexicon of filthy boo-words to describe the yuckiness of life, from septic and squalid to stercoraceous and pediculous, but none carries the precise sense of excrementitious increment. This lost word from the Roman Catholic Church appears to have been used mostly, if not exclusively, in religious literature. But our secular world is full of things increasing in filthiness, so this is a useful word to use when rising filth makes your gorge and vocab rise.

As in: 'Your eating habits are insordescent, Philip: wear an apron.'

JANIFORM

Two-faced. Like Janus, the Ancient Roman god of gateways and doorways.

Janus presided over all beginnings, which Romans believed crucial to the success of any undertaking, and he gave his name to the first month of the year. He had two faces, one looking forwards and one backwards, just as every door looks two ways. The doors of his temple were open in times of war, and closed in (infrequent) times of peace.

Sydney Smith, 1814: 'The statue was to be janiform, with Playfair's face on one side and Stewart's on the other.'

Bit of a comedown from God to an obscure pejorative epithet. Certainly a more elegant insult than 'two-faced'.

As in: 'I wonder whether you are not a bit janiform in your congratulations.'

JEHU

A reckless driver, Jehu was a King of Israel in the ninth century BC, famous for both his furious chariot driving and for his extermination of the worshippers of Baal. His eponym comes from II Kings, ix:20: 'The driving is like the driving of Jehu the son of Nimshi; for he driveth furiously.' Rhyme it, generously, with 'See few'.

Oliver Goldsmith, 'The Bee: No. 5', (Reverie), 1759: 'He assured the Coachman that his baggage was perfectly light. But Jehu was inflexible.'

John Dryden, *The Medal*, 1682: 'But this new Jehu spurs the hot-mouth'd horse.'

Jehu is not the only eponym for silly petrolheads. Phaëton is another. In ancient Greek mythology, he was the son of Helios, the Sun God. To prove his paternity, Phaëton asked for permission to drive his father's sun chariot across the sky for one day. Helios was fearful for his safety and tried to dissuade him, but nothing could quell Phaëton's enthusiasm, and Helios had to stand by his word. The four horses bolted. Zeus was forced to thunderbolt Phaëton to save the world from total combustion. Phaëton came to mean a carriage, as well as its reckless driver.

As in: 'May I sit in the back rather than the front suicide seat, my dear Jehu?'

JEJUNE

Not so much lost as mispronounced and misattributed. Its primary modern meaning is insipid, meagre, short of worthwhile content. Pronounce it, roughly, to rhyme with 'Eh, June?'

Because of its similarity to the French for 'young', it is often misapplied to mean primitive, inchoate, childish. In fact, it is an adaptation of the Latin *jejunus*: fasting, and it originally came into English, in the sixteenth and seventeenth centuries, to mean just that: hungry. Thence it took off, to mean deficient in substantial qualities, unsatisfying to the mind or soul and, especially of speech or writing, vacuous.

George Berkeley's *Commonplace Book*, 1705: 'The short jejune way in mathematics will not do in metaphysics.'

William Blackstone, *Commentaries on the Laws of England*, 1758: 'He gives what seems a very jejune and unsatisfactory reason.'

You may infer from this that 'jejune' is a word for lawyers and philosophers, not poets and soap operas. It is a sharp, superior word.

As in: 'I enjoy the rhetoric in your essay on *Twelfth Night*, Charlotte, but I find its argument jejune.'

JETTATORE

Somebody who is/brings bad luck. A Jonah. Even though she or he is the first person to be chucked off the life raft in dire straits, when supplies run low, the 'jettatore' is in no way related to 'jettison' or 'jetsam'. It is an adaptation of the Italian *iettatura*, the evil eye: bad luck. The 'jettatore' is somebody who possesses the evil eye, a bringer of bad luck. Pronounce, roughly, to rhyme with 'Bet a Tory'.

Andrew Lang, *Books and Bookmen*, 1892: 'The superstitious might have been excused for crediting him with the gift of jettatura – of the evil eye.'

The (Glasgow) Herald, 1921: 'This simple remedy is much in use throughout Italy today as an antidote to the evil power of the Jettatore.'

We live in an age of credulity; think of all our bizarre cults and con(wo)men in religion and politics. So we have room for an elegant word for the bringer of bad luck, provided that we recognise we can make our own luck, even King Lear: 'It is the stars, / The stars above us that govern our conditions.' Up to a point, Lord Kent.

As in: 'Of course you are not a jettatore, Maxwell. Why do you suppose you are always chosen first?'

<u>JOBATION</u>

A rebuke, jaw-jaw, scolding, ticking-off; especially one of a lengthy, tedious and generally arse-aching character. The action of the verb 'to Jobe', in allusion to the reproofs addressed to Job by his sanctimonious 'friends'. Dialectically, usually pronounced and spelt 'jawbation', as though it were derived from 'jaw-jawing'.

Thomas Hughes, *Tom Brown at Oxford*, 1861: 'Don't be angry at my jobation; but write me a long answer.'

John Smith, letter in Granville's *Reminiscences*, 1687: 'I had far rather venture to be liable to a jobation for not having done my part.'

This schoolboy slang, with its reference to the most poetic book in the Old Testament, deserves resurrection. Bertie Wooster, who won a prize for scriptural knowledge at his Prepper, would surely approve.

As in: 'Thank you for your helpful remarks about my socks, Major Jarvis. I really must remember to get my wife to give you one of her famous jobations.'

JOCOSERIOUS

Half jocular, half serious; partly in jest and partly in earnest; blending jokes and serious matters. Hence 'jocoseriosity'. This word is to some extent self-referential. It looks like a serious word, but it's quite silly. It wears its meaning in its spelling, as plain as a pikestaff (though why pikestaffs are plain is a topic for another day). A combined form of the Latin *jocus*, a joke, plus 'serious'. Pronounce to rhyme, sort of, with 'Mock, O Beery Puss!'

Edward Johnson, *Browning Society Papers*, 1885: 'Our own poet has lately characterised himself as a jocoserious genius; and in fact this jocoseriosity seems of a similar quality as the eironeia of the Greek.'

Jocoseriosity can be seen as a quality of the British character, which finds humour in unpromising situations. It's better to laugh than to cry. Discuss. Compare with 'agathokakological', consisting of both good and evil, another grand Janus word that likes to eat its cake and have it too.

We need a word to describe the native habit of wanting to have it both ways.

As in: 'I am being only jocoserious, Sophie, when I say that we need to do an hour of algebra tonight.'

KECK

To make a sound as though one were about to vomit. Presumably echoic. Cf. Gammer Gurton's Needle, 1553: 'Till I made her olde wesen to answere again, keck.' Rhyme with check, heck and peck.

A multipurpose word: in its various senses it also effortlessly manages to describe to retch, to feel an inclination to vomit, to 'shoot a tiger', to reject (food, medicine etc.) with loathing and, figuratively, to express strong dislike or disgust. Compare and contrast 'nauseant' and 'vomiturient'.

Jonathan Swift, letter, 1710: 'I have taken a whole box of pills, and keckt at them every night.'

Charles Lamb, byline Elia, *The London Magazine*, 'Imperfect Sympathies', 1821: 'If they can sit with us at table, why do they keck at our cookery?'

Puking is an unpleasant syndrome both for the kecker and for everybody in range. Babies do it, while learning to keep their food down.

Young men, prone to kecking because of drinking too much, have created a number of euphemisms: technicolor yawn, chunder, feed the fishes etc., ad nauseam.

We should revive this word as a useful and onomatopoeic cover for its retching wretched unpleasantness.

As in: 'I was proposed and seconded for membership of the Gawwick, but the members kecked at me.'

LABILE

Unstable; liable to change. Prone to fall into error or sin. In theology, liable to fall from innocence. Apt to slip away, slippery. Now mostly used in chemistry and physics: prone to undergo displacement in position or change in nature, form or chemical composition; unstable. Rhyme, roughly, with 'grey bile'.

The social scientists appropriated 'labile' in the hope that this esoteric term would lend their writings a mask of scientific prestige. They use 'labile' to refer to personality or emotion. Cf. and contrast the sociological use of 'paradigm'.

George Cheyne, *An Essay in Regimen*, 1740: 'Creatures being finite and free, must necessarily, by their Nature, be labile, fallible and peccable.'

Thence, Lord Salisbury, *The Popular Science Monthly*, 1894: 'The genius of Lord Kelvin has recently discovered what he terms a labile state of equilibrium.'

'Labile' suggests, nicely, 'labial' and 'nubile'. So it is unfortunate that 'labile', in the jargon of social science, means moody and temperamental.

As in: 'Claire, I fear that on skates I am labile rather than stable. Eheu!'

LANT

To mix urine with ale in order to make it stronger. Rhyme with 'rant' and 'bant' and 'elephant'. As a noun, lant means urine, especially stale urine used for various industrial purposes, such as beefing up beer. Alias 'chamber-lye'. The Romans used to collect urine in tanks in the street for use as starch.

M.W., *The Marriage Broker*, 1662: 'My Hostess taking will be very small, Although her lanted ale be ne'er so strong.'

Glapthorne, *Wit in Constable*, 1640: 'Your nose by its complexion does betray / Your frequent drinking country Ale with lant in't.'

One hopes that practice of beefing up beer with pee has fallen into obsolescence in these days of obsessive hygiene, but it is still a useful word to tease the landlord in the public bar.

As in: 'I congratulate you on your ale, Margaret. My guess is that you have lanted it well.'

LAPIDATE

To stone to death. To throw stones at; to pelt with stones. Rhyme with 'happy fête' (or, more appropriately, 'crappy fate').

The existence of this word in English indicates that the custom existed when some parts of the 'civilised' world were as barbaric as contemporary Iran. *Lapis* is Latin for a stone. *Lapidare* was the ancient Roman practice: when they were not executing criminals and other inconveniences to the State or ruling class by flinging them off the Tarpeian Rock, they lapidated them.

Byron, *To Moore*, 1816: 'Whom the mob quartered and lapidated.'

Lapidation after quartering sounds to me a work of supererogation. Alas: we still need this word to describe the horror in the modern as well as the ancient world.

As in: 'Yes, Mrs Pecksniff; the children do spend a lot of time reading. They used to have a proper hobby – lapidation – but they have trouble finding a suitable subject. Perhaps you could oblige?'

LEEP

To wash with cowdung and water.

Eh? Surely not, ed.?

An adaptation of the Urdu (and Hindi) *lipna*. This makes me wonder whether the compilers of *The Oxford English Dictionary* have a different definition of 'wash' than we do. But no. To wash: 'To cleanse, remove the dirt from (something) by affusion or immersion in water.' No mention of cowpats, but note the origins of the word, where cow dung is a multipurpose commodity for everything from fuel to washing. And as dung goes, cow dung is a great deal less offensive than that of carnivores such as human beings or dogs.

Kipling, *The Second Jungle Book*, 1895: 'The big wicker-chest, leeped with cow-dung.'

Opportunities for use of this Anglo-Indian word may be occasional, but leep leaps off the screen as a learned and unprovocative word for use with the car-wash at the garage.

As in: 'Thanks for washing the old crate, Jerry. You have leeped it like a true pro.'

LEESE

To be a loser. This word has as many meanings as forms. It has been used to signify 'to lose', in several senses; to part with or be parted from, by misadventure, through change in conditions etc.; to be deprived of; to cease to possess; to fail to preserve or maintain; to fail to secure; to destroy or bring to ruin etc. All fine words, but all have synonyms, and add little to the toolbox of English. But we have no other word that means 'to be a loser'. Rhyme with 'cease'.

Its roots are lost in the jungles of Old English and Teutonic, but a sound guess is to trace them back to Greek *luein*, Latin *solvere*, to loosen.

Richard Hakluyt, *The Principal Navigations, Voyages, and Discoveries of the English Nation*, 1599: 'Whereby the Empire of Constantinople leeseth, and is like to leese.'

Philemon Holland, *Camden's Britannia*, 1610: 'All things [are] to follow in an easy and expedite course if you win, but all against you, if you leese.'

It is worth reviving this lost word to fill a vacant pigeonhole in the lexicon.

As in: 'You may not enjoy netball, Juliet, but join in, cheer up, do not leese.'

LETABUND

Full of joy. Joyful. Adaptation of the Latin *laetabundus*, from *laetari*, to give joy. Pronounce, pushing it a bit, to rhyme with 'Peter hound'.

William Stewart, *The Chronicles of Scotland*, 1535: 'Of whom came this noble King Edmund, / As bird on brier was blythe and letabund.'

It is agreeable to recover a happy word with the usually unhappy ending -bund. Most words ending in 'bund' are gloomy. Furibund: the end of good humour; moribund: the end of life; cummerbund: the end of elegance; and Balkansprachbund: the grouping of linguistic similarities among the Balkan languages. So let's hear it for happy letabund.

Joyful, surprisingly, also has a Latin root: 'gaudium', meaning joy. And still, as late as 1945, in Lou Shelly's *Hepcats Jive Talk*, we hear of being 'conjubilant'; rejoicing with somebody else. It is a rum concept, as to rejoice on one's own is not really letabund. And how about 'felicificability': the capacity for happiness, a sesquipedalian word for a happy quality?

As in: 'I am letabund to watch you dance, but to join in would not increase my felicificability.'

MACARONIC

A burlesque verse form in which vernacular words are introduced into a Latin context with Latin terminations and Latin constructions. A jocular medley of Latin with other tongues.

Done well, macaronics can be amusing. Overdone, they can become a bore. Every schoolchild used to know A. D. Godley's verse, which begins: 'What is this that roareth thus? / Can it be a motor bus? / Yes, the smell and hideous hum / *Indicat motorem bum* ...' That is macaronic.

Pronounce, mechanically, to rhyme with 'catatonic'. The root is 'macaroon', now used for a biscuit with an almond flavour.

Italian poet Teofilo Folengo, 'Merlinus Cocaius' (1517), described macaroni as a coarse, wheaten peasant dish. Hence 'macaroon' came to mean a coarse, doltish fellow.

Uncle Sam, according to Boswell, 1778: 'Macaronick verses are verses made out of a mixture of various languages.'

So, if you find your galootish nephew eating a macaroon, you could make a comment about the persistence of cannibalism.

As in: 'Your Latin prose, Daniel, is macaronically inspired.'

MAFFLE

To stammer, speak indistinctly or mumble. A 'mafflard' is a stammering or blundering fool. Cf. the early modern Dutch *maffelen*, to move the jaws. The English word has a wide dialectal currency in several senses. Rhyme with 'raffle'.

1603: 'Those disciples who would needs stut, stammer and maffle as Aristotle did.'

1450: 'The Church of Chester, which crieth, Alas! That to such a mafflard married she was.'

Mafflards have had a rough time for thousands of years, being the recipients of more misguided attempts to 'cure' them than any other group, with the possible exception of sinistrals (the left-handed). In the Middle Ages some thought that the tongue itself was the problem, and attempts were made to torture the offending organ into correctitude with pins and hot irons.

My precentor at school, who coached us to sing in chapel, was a terrible mafflard in speech, but sang like a nightingale.

As in: 'Don't maffle, Ollie. Which do you prefer to do: floodlit rugby or revision of quadratic equations?'

MALESUETE

With bad habits. Accustomed to poor habits or customs. Adaptation of the quasi-Latin *male* (ill) plus *suetus* (accustomed).

Nathan (or Nathaniel) Bailey, *Universal Etymological Dictionary* (1727), a popular forerunner and source for Sam Johnson's dictionary: 'Malesuete – That has contracted an ill Habit or Custom.'

This is an elegant word to describe the inelegant minor flaws and foibles that afflict almost all of us, and our best friends hesitate to tell us about. Nothing as tragic as killing one's father and marrying one's mother, but minor bad habits such as picking one's nose and eating the snot, or boasting about one's children, or cutting one's toenails in public.

As in: 'To grab the last éclair on the plate, without even offering it to your sister, could be deemed by the punctilious a tad malesuete, Lucy.'

MALISON

A curse or malediction. As a verb: to curse; to pronounce a malediction upon. Rhyme with 'Rally's on'. Adaptation of the Old French *maleison*. Truncated adaptation of the Latin *male* (evil) plus *dictio* (speech).

Allan Ramsay, *Lucky Spence*, 1721: 'My malison light ilka day / On them that drink and dinna pay.'

Adam King, *Canisius' Catechism*, 1588: 'To malison any, by giving them to the devil, in wishing them sickness, death or any evil.'

Walter Scott, *Marmion*, 1808: 'A minstrel's malison is said.'

Also, a plague or torment. A cat malison is somebody (something) who is cruel to cats, such as a Jack Russell. A horse malison is one who is cruel to horses.

The Latinate 'malison' sounds more terrible than the Old English 'curse', which is of problematic etymology.

As in: 'A malison on these irregular verbs, Hugh, but grit teeth and heads down.'

MAMMOTHREPT

A spoilt brat. Rhyme, deviously, with 'Ammo kept'. From the Greek for 'a child raised by his (or her) granny'. Its first recorded use is by St Augustine, which the *OED* finds puzzling since he knew no Greek. Perhaps he took the word from Silver Latin, a language with which he was comfortable.

John Davies, *Holy Rood*, 1609: 'And for we are the Mammothrepts of Sin, / Cross us with Christ, to wean our joys therein.'

Ben Jonson, *Cynthia's Revels*, 1599: Amo: 'How like you it, sir?' Hed: 'Very well in troth.' Amo: 'But very well? O, you are a mere mammothrept in judgment.'

The waters were muddied by critics misunderstanding this quotation and defining 'mammothrept' as a severe critic. For example, Brathwait, *Smoking Age*, 1617: 'Or what strict Mammothrept that man should be, / Who has done Chaucer such an injury.'

There is room in our word-cupboard for a posh word for a spoilt, unruly brat. There are plenty around. Except of course among your children and mine, darling.

As in: 'You must share your chocolate éclairs, Grace, or I shall put you down as a mere mammothrept.'

MARITALITY

Excessive affection of a wife for her husband. The correlative of uxoriousness, which is the excessive affection of a husband for his wife. Neither quality is common in our age. This is an adaptation of the Latin *maritus*, a husband.

William Taylor, *The Monthly Magazine*, 1812: 'The uxoriousness of the husband was in neither case requited by the maritality of the wife.'

Although the quality is rare, and the word will not often be required, the Latinate expression is typically more economical than any Anglo-Saxon paraphrase. The adjective is 'maritorious', which sounds almost familiar.

As in: 'Elizabeth's maritality is meritorious but ostentatious.'

MATAEOTECHNY

An unprofitable science. Adaptation of the Greek *mataios*, vain, useless, plus *technee*, an art or skill.

Isaac Newton, *Lemnie's Complex*, 1576: 'Such a peevish practice, and unnecessary mataeotechny.'

Gregory in Stephen Rigaud, *Correspondence of Scientific Men of the Seventeenth Century*, 1675: 'I am much mistaken if to force an equality between a negative and affirmative root be not a mere useless mataeotechny.'

Astrology is the classic mataeotechny, but if it is authentic science (knowledge obtained by observation and experiment), it cannot be useless.

As in: 'Tegestology [collecting beer mats] can be defined as a mataeotechny in the extreme acceptance of the word, Richard, without much risk of terminological inexactitude.'

MATERTERAL

Having the characteristics or qualities of an aunt. Humorously pedantic. Adaptation of the (obscurish) Latin *matertera*, a maternal aunt. Rhyme (etymologically and roughly) with 'Greater feral'.

1823: 'With maternal and materteral anxiety.'

1874: 'A kindly materterine [variant] message.'

It is surprising, and perhaps Woosterish-sexist, that 'avuncular' has had such a success, implying slightly Old Bufferish generosity and good humour, whereas 'materteral' has been dumped on the lexical compost heap, along with the fearful aunts of Bertie, Saki and Kipling. It languishes there, beside 'consobrinal' (having the relationship of a cousin), an unlucky familial word that has been neglected.

Aunts can be just as kind as uncles (and more so). Time to revive dear old materteral.

As in: 'You are truly materteral, dear Judy, to be so kind to our boys.'

MAWWORM

A hypocrite with pretensions of sanctity. The mawworm is biologically a worm infesting the intestines of man and other animals. Hence it became Mawworm, a character in Bickerstaffe's play, *The Hypocrite* (1769). Generally it came to mean a pious fraud.

George Eliot, *Middlemarch*, 1872: 'He would be the very Mawworm of bachelors who pretended ...'

Robert Buchanan, *Coming Terror*, 1891: 'The Scapin of Politics walks hand-in-hand with the Mawworm of Morality.'

You might ask who needs Mawworm when we have Pecksniff and Uriah Heep. English is rich in epithets for toadies, sycophants, freeloaders, kowtowers, creeping Jesuses, spaniels, bumsuckers and parasites – ad nauseam. But in an election year, the more synonyms for pious gits the better.

As in: 'Pass the sick-bag, Annabel; I have had enough of these Mawworms on party political broadcasts.'

MICROPHILY

The friendship of a 'small' man with a great one. Love between people who are not equal in intelligence or status. Ropily derived from the Greek for 'small' plus 'friendship'.

Daniel Tuvil, *Essaies Politicke, and Morall*, 1608: 'So likewise, where there is a disproportion either in means, or minds, there can be no other friendship than that Microphily, which Plato had with Dionysius the Tyrant.'

Friendship (or love) ought to be blind to status or money; alas, history is against this romantic notion. Think of Falstaff (the clever one) and Prince Harry; Diana, Princess of Wales, and the Prince of Wales; Cardinal Wolsey and Henry VIII; Arthur Miller and Marilyn Monroe.

As in: 'It is an honour to be invited to lunch with the chairman, but beware of microphily.'

MINIONETTE

Small and pretty. Adaptation of the French *mignon-ette*, the diminutive of *mignon*, English 'minion', which originally meant a darling, favourite, or beloved object. But minionette remains a lost hurrah-word.

Horace Walpole, letter, 1749: 'His minionette face.'

It is an Anglo-Saxon prejudice to prefer the tall to the short. Remember Hermia in *A Midsummer Night's Dream*? '"Little" again? Nothing but "low" and "little"? Why will you suffer her to flout me thus?' Lysander: 'Get you gone, you dwarf; you minimus...'

The principal consequence of being over 6ft tall is to hit your head and scramble your brains. So let's hear it for Thumbelina, Lilliputians, Borrowers, Munchkins and our minionettes.

As in: 'Stand not on tiptoe, dear minionette: you are perfect as you are.'

MISANDRY

Hatred of males. Rhyme, approximately, with 'my hands dry'. Adaptation of the Greek *misein*, to hate, and *andros* (male), man.

Scrutiny, 1946: 'In the absence of feminine precedents, she [sc. Beatrice in *Much Ado About Nothing*] could do no better than what she very sensibly does do: follow masculine example and answer to their affected misogyny with the affectation of misandry.'

Why is misandry far less common today than its partner, misogyny? Can it be that women are naturally more generous than men? Surely not. Oh well, OK, probably. Let us avoid both hateful words in practice, but keep misandry in our locker for special occasions.

Does the fact that there are so many more words for hate than love in the English lexicon say something unattractive about human nature? Probably.

As in: 'God knows, women have had centuries of misogyny to endure, but let us not allow true-bluestocking feminism to decline into misandry.'

MONDO

Very much, extremely. Considerable, huge. Slang, originally and mainly US. A word of bizarre etymology: Italian *mondo* (Latin *mundus*) means 'world'.

In 1962 an Italian film appeared called *Mondo Cane*, literally 'World of a Dog', which was given the English title *A Dog's Life*. It depicted eccentric forms of human behaviour, and 'mondo' came to be used in (often mock-Italian) pastiches on the film's name, denoting bizarre words (e.g., 'Mondo Weirdo'). In these expressions 'mondo' was reinterpreted as an adverb meaning 'very' (probably helped by a vague resemblance to the Spanish *mucho*), and, Mondo Bingo, its new career was born. That's the way the words and the world go.

As in: 'He's so mondo cool, even though he's not British and doesn't have spiked hair.'

MOUNTEBANK

A travelling salesman. An itinerant quack who, from an elevated platform, appealed to his audience by means of stories, tricks and juggling, in which he was often assisted by a professional clown or fool. From the Italian for 'mount-the-bench'. Cf. 'saltimbanco', which is derived from the same principle – *saltatio* is Latin for a jump. Do not confuse with saltimbocca, the veal dish that 'jumps in the mouth'. Pronounce to rhyme, roughly, with 'Count the bank'.

John Gay, *The Shepherd's Week*, 1714: 'The mountebank now treads the stage, and sells / His pills, his balsams, and his ague-spells.'

Attributively, Jonathan Swift, *Concerning the Strange and Deplorable Frenzy of John Dennis*, 1713: 'He hath told others that he had seen me upon a mountebank stage in Moorfields.'

The charlatan who wishes to display his wares and con the susceptible these days does not need to climb on a bench. He solicits appearances on daytime television chat shows.

As in: 'Where does the *Today* programme find these mountebanks and saltimbancos to make me cut myself while shaving?'

MULIEBRITY

Womanhood. The characteristics or qualities of a woman. Adaptation of the Latin *mulier*, a woman; hence *muliebritas*, womanhood.

Oliver Wendell Holmes, 'Autocrat of the Breakfast-Table', in instalments in *Atlantic Monthly*, 1857–58: 'The second of the ravishing voices had so much woman in it – muliebrity, as well as femineity.'

The distinction that O.W.H. is making is between the essence and the profession of being a woman.

Francis Bret Harte, *Phyllis of the Sierras*, 1888: 'This tall woman possessed a refined muliebrity superior to mere liberality of contour.'

As in: 'A bit more muliebrity, Edith, and a bit less feminism.'

MUMPSIMUS

An old fogey. One who obstinately adheres to old ways, in spite of clear evidence that they are wrong; an ignorant and bigoted opponent of reform.

Who can they be thinking of? The etymology alludes to the story, recorded from 1517, of an illiterate English priest who, when corrected for misreading *quod in ore mumpsimus* in the Mass, replied: 'I will not change my old *mumpsimus* for your new *sumpsimus*.'

The word can also mean a custom or notion obstinately adhered to, however unreasonable it is shown to be.

John Keble, *Pusey*, 1862: 'I still hold to my old mumpsimus that the Prayer Book being what it is we cannot be unchurched by mere abuse or default of discipline.'

Neophiliacs are more fashionable (and irritating?) today than mumpsimuses. But this is a pretty word with which to hoist fogeys by their old cacoethes.

As in: 'Don't be such a mumpsimus, Paul: soya milk does not damage your semen.'

NEPENTHE

A drink or drug supposed to bring forgetfulness of trouble and grief.

In the fourth book of *The Odyssey*, the Egyptian Queen gives Helen '*nepenthes pharmakon*': an 'anti-sorrow drug'. Deconstructionist scholars suggest that this could have been an opium derivative such as laudanum, but they are making a category mistake, and trying to herd a Cheshire Cat. *The Odyssey* is an epic, not a catalogue of pharmacology.

Lord Chesterfield, *World*, 1754: 'Gallons of the Nepenthe would be lost on him. The more he drinks, the duller he grows.'

Percy Bysshe Shelley, *The Triumph of Life*, 1822: 'In her right hand she bore a crystal glass, / Mantling with bright Nepenthe.'

This is a perfect name for a new liqueur. Besides, there is room for a word to describe something that reduces the tribulations of this wicked world.

As in: 'A glass of my usual nepenthe, Andrew; you had better make it a double. I have just had a letter from Mr Taxman.'

NEPOTATION

Extravagance, prodigality, squandering one's money on riotous living. *Blount's Glossary*, 1656: 'Wasting or riotousness.' Adaptation of the participle stem of the Latin *nepotari*, to be prodigal, squander.

Peter Hawkins, *The Way of the World*, 1854: 'I can no longer afford to finance your pernocturnal nepotations, Harry: you must not try to outprodigal the Prodigal Son.'

Do not confuse with nepotism, which is favouritism for relatives – originally fondness for nephews, specifically papal fondness for illegitimate sons referred to as 'nephews'. Latin *nepos* means nephew.

Edward Freeman, *The Norman Conquest*, 1876: 'This nepotism of the Bishop who made a maintenance for his kinsfolk out of the estates of the Church.'

All Souls College, Oxford was founded on nepotism for the founder's kin.

Fun and generosity are virtues: nepotation is their shady excess; a useful lost word for our prodigal age.

As in: 'As it is your birthday, Lawrence, we should have a family nepotation. But tomorrow it is back to homework, auld claes and porritch.'

NICE

'Nice' is not lost. But it's a chameleon word. There is no need to revive it; but it would be nice if we could pin its meaning down.

It came into English in the thirteenth century from the Latin *nescius*: ignorant; not-knowing. It has meant everything from 'no-better-than-she-should-be' (women), to 'pedantically precise' (men). In many examples from the sixteenth and seventeenth centuries it is difficult to tell in what (nice) sense the writer intended. Since the eighteenth century it has morphed into the general (vacuous) hurrah-word, meaning agreeable. There is evidence that it is changing colour again into an imprecise and ironic boo-word.

Israel Zangwill, *Children of the Ghetto*, 1892: 'Well, you're a nice friend of his, I must say.'

When a word has so many different and opposing meanings, it would be nice if it died of shame. It won't.

As in: 'It would be nice, Stephen, if you would explain the nice sense in which you are using the adjective nice.'

<u>NIDDERING</u>

A base coward or wretch. Rhyme with 'Hid her ring'. Also in predicative use, it developed into an adjective as base, cowardly, vile.

And it was coined by a mistake. The word is derived erroneously from the Viking *nithing*, a vile coward, which occurs on a runic stone at Aarhus in Denmark. The bish occured in a printed text of William of Malmesbury in 1596. The printer misread the thorn (the Anglo-Saxon letter for 'th') as a D.

Walter Scott (that keen reviver of lost words) passim, as in *Ivanhoe*, 1819: 'Threatening to stigmatise those who staid at home as niddering ... On pain of being held faithless, man-sworn and niddering.'

After such a muddled transmission, the old word deserves resurrection. It sounds more robust than coward, and fills the mouth better.

As in: 'No niddering gets to play at scrummy as you do, Simon.'

NITID

Bright, shining, polished, glossy – in literal or figurative senses. Rhymes, approximately, with 'Sit, kid.' Adaptation of the Latin *nitere*, to shine; whence *nitidus*, shiny.

James Thomson, *The Seasons, Spring*, 1728: 'The nitid Hues, / Which speck them o'er.'

Sydney Smith, 1823: 'Forth from his bill-case this votary of Plutus took his nitid Newlands.' A Bank of England note, eponym of Abraham Newland, chief cashier of the Bank of England from 1782 to 1807.

Hester Thrale (Mrs Piozzi), 1794: 'Una resembles a pearl, loveliest in the strong and open daylight, where all her nitid beauties show most clearly.'

English, the omniverous tongue, has plenty of words for shining, from luminous to scintillating, but we can always use a new, short and ... nitid one.

As in: 'I adore your nitid Saturday face, Josie.'

NOCENT

Harmful, injurious, hurtful. Adaptation of the Latin *nocens*, *nocent-*, the present participle of *nocere*, to hurt. Rhyme with 'No Sent'.

'Nocuous' is another virtually lost word, with the same etymology and similar meaning: noxious, hurtful; venomous, poisonous. Rhyme, asymmetrically this time (with a short 'o', as in 'hot'), with 'Mock you, Gus!'

John Milton, *Paradise Lost*, 1667: 'Nor yet in horrid Shade or dismal Den, / Not nocent yet.'

Carl Sofus Lumholtz (the Norwegian explorer and ethnographer), *Among Cannibals*, 1889: 'This change is due to a nocuous kind of grass, namely the dreaded spear-grass.'

Observe that these are the roots for our two common words, 'innocent' and 'innocuous'. For profound psychological or linguistic reasons, do we have a natural preference for words that have been negatived by prefix? Come on, pull the other one. If so, let's hear it for the neologism to describe the flatlands of Wapping: 'unundulating'.

As in: 'To mix beer with wine is not simply nocent, Ben, it is positively nocuous.'

NOCEUR

One who stays up late at night: a reveller, rake, Hooray Henry or libertine. Odd (or is it?) how there is a Roget of words for a cad: Casanova, Don Juan, Lothario, satyr, whoremonger, dirty old man…

Noceur is unique in its denotation. It is differentiated from the rest of the crowd in seedy macs or gaudy weskits by being the only one that specifies that the cad in question stays up late at night.

'The French noceur is only too pleased to show himself in the company of some well-known horizontale.'

There are some contexts when noceur hits the bull's-eye rather than a magpie.

As in: 'Drink up. Time to go home, Princess Beatrice. Your friend is a notorious noceur.'

NOSOPOETIC

No, not 'not so poetic', but 'producing disease, unhygienic, infected'. *Nosos* is Greek for disease. *Poe(e)tic* is Greek for 'making'.

John Arbuthnot, *An Essay on Air*, 1733: 'I shall make a few Observations upon the Qualities of the Air, so far as they are Nosopoetick, that is, have a Power of producing Disease.'

We have space for a word to describe the several diseases, such as hayfever, that flesh is heir (air) to. For it is broader than unhygienic, infectious, poisonous. Yuk!

And it is a useful double-edged irony to deploy when the wealthy Plushington-Brassnecks are showing off pictures of their Tuscan villa, reports of their child's brilliance at Dotheboys Hall, new Porsche, bathroom tiles, seaside cottage, sunken garden. 'How exquisitely nosopoetic!' you exclaim.

Note other 'noso-' words, such as 'nosophobia'.

In 1889, *The Lancet* had: 'Nosophobia is certainly much more frequent in man, probably because women act as nurses, and consequently have no fear of infection.'

As in: 'Hold your breath in this wild Scotch Mist from Arran, Alison: I fear that it is nosopoetic.'

NOYADE

The mass execution of persons by drowning, as practised in revolutionary France, perfected at Nantes in 1794. Adaptation of the Latin *necare*, to put to death (in late Latin 'to drown'). You shut up some 150 people (preferably aristos or other undesirables) in the hold of a ship, which was then scuttled in the Loire.

Thomas Babington Macaulay, essay, 1835: 'Then came revolutionary tribunals, guillotinades, noyades, fusillades.'

Occasions to use this word literally are rare, but it is a good lost word for jocular use. As you see the first form leaving for swimming lessons in the school bus, you could shout: 'Have a good old noyade then, little darlings.' They know your penchant for lost words, and smile tolerantly, while turning their full attention to the task of defenestrating their teacher.

As in: 'OK, I will come to the municipal pool with you, Robert. But promise: no water fights or attempts at noyades.'

NUDNIK

Someone incessantly tedious or pestering. A crashing bore. Derived from the Russian *nudnyi* meaning 'tedious or boring'. Also shares close relations with the identical Yiddish word meaning someone who is a pest. Its first appearance was in the *New Republic* when referring to a New York bistro whose clientele were the complete antithesis of its vibrant tradition.

New Republic, 1947: 'The patrons of New York's Ruban Bleu are as boorish a collection of nudni(c)ks as ever assembled in a public place.'

New York, 1972: 'Too many of our nudnik moviegoers dread the prospect of sharing their pleasures with the plain folks.'

There is a discrepancy relating to nudnik as a term of endearment, as paradoxically exercised by Paul Durst in his book, *Badge of Infamy*, 1968: 'Nudnik is a kind of insulting endearment – a sort of lovable nitwit.'

There is room for a word that permits covert sledging of tiresome pests and combines fashionable colloquialism with euphemistic aggression.

As in: 'Don't invite him, Gregory, he is an insufferable nudnik.'

NYMPHOLEPSY

Not, in its primary sense, ungovernable lust for young females, but a state of rapture supposed to be inspired in men by nymphs; hence, a frenzy of emotion, especially inspired by something unattainable. From the Greek for 'caught by nymphs'. Rhyme, ludicrously, with 'Hymn to Pepsi'.

Byron, *Childe Harold*, 1818: 'A young Aurora of the air, / The nympholepsy of some fond despair.'

De Quincey, *Recollected Lakes*, 1839: 'He languished with a sort of despairing nympholepsy after intellectual pleasures.'

A sufferer is a 'nympholept'.

Shelley, letter, 1818: 'I hope your nympholeptic tale is not abandoned.'

You could use 'nympholepsy' to describe the passion of a dedicated philatelist for a misprinted Penny Black, or of a Jeremy Petrolhead for an impossibly dear Bugatti, or of a classical scholar for a lost play of Euripides. Or, let's face it, of a lover for his mistress, as in Nabokov, *Lolita*, 1955: 'The science of nympholepsy is a precise science. Actual contact would do it in one second flat. An interspace of a millimetre would do it in ten.' Was the logophile confusing the word with 'nymphomaniac' here?

Worth reviving for crazy enthusiasms?

As in: 'Do you not think that your passion for Berwick Rangers is nympholepsy, Jamie?'

OBLOQUY

Evil-speaking, directed against a person or thing; abuse, detraction, calumny, slander. Also, with 'an' or in the plural, an abusive speech or utterance. Thence, public condemnation, abuse or detraction, evil fame, bad repute; a reproach or disgrace. Adaptation of the late Latin *obloquium*, a contradiction; *obloqui*, to speak against, contradict, gainsay. Rhyme, with difficulty, with 'Bob, rock we?'

Shakespeare, *Henry VI*, Part I, 1591: 'And did upbraid me with my father's death; / Which obloquy set bars before my tongue.'

This word falls somewhere in between 'opprobrium' and 'odium'. I tried to invent a sentence using all three to compare and contrast the different meanings but fell headlong into obluctation, obmutescence and obfuscation.

Although it has many close cognates, 'obloquy' has several sharp meanings of its own that no other word replicates. So let us revive this lost word; but use it only when strictly justified.

As in: 'I want you to take this as constructive criticism not obloquy, Jonathan.'

OPSIGAMY

Marrying late in life; elderly Eros; archaic Cupid. Greek *opse/i* means 'late'; *gamos*, marriage. 'Opsigamia', late marriage; 'opsigamos', somebody who married/marries late in life. Rhyme, just about, with 'Flopsy Mammy'.

John McCulloch, *The Highlands and Western Islands of Scotland*, 1824: 'Nor is there any danger of Donald's being flogged for opsigamy by the Highland nymphs as the Spartans were of old.'

Do not confuse opsigamist with opsimath (somebody who begins to learn late in life). The opsigamist has evidently learned nothing at all.

British customs of matrimony are on the cusp, and the whole country's in a state of chassis. There is room in our word store for this elegant word to describe the modern tendency to marry late, if ever.

As in: 'I am delighted at your opsigamy, Solomon; better luck second time round.'

OPSIMATH

Somebody who learns late in life. One who begins to learn or study late in life. A laggard learner. Adapted from the Greek *opse*, late, plus *manthanein*, to learn; *mathee*, learning. Pronounce to rhyme, roughly, with 'You're a Popsy, Cath'.

Church Times, 1883: 'Those who gave the name were not simple enough to think that even an opsimath was not something better than a contented dunce.'

The London Periodical Saturday Review, 1883: '[He] is what the Greeks called an opsimath; not ignorant, but a laggard in learning.'

Even the brightest of us have subjects in which our knowledge is limited, or blank; for example, classical Sanskrit. We should all be opsimaths: to strive, to seek, to find, and not to yield.

Good word when writing school reports: 'English, Maths, Science, Geography, PE and effort were admittedly a little disappointing, even for him. But he has all the necessary background to make a future for himself as an opsimath.'

As in: 'In his retirement Mark is learning Sanskrit as an opsimath.'

PALAEOLATRY

Worship of, or excessive reverence for, what is ancient. A rum kind of nostalgia for the past, extending far back to a time before the person who feels it was born. Could a lover of lost words be described as a semantic palaeolater? Greek *palaeo* means ancient; *latrein* is to worship. Rhymes, approximately, with 'Pal, I love flattery'.

The Athenaeum, 1887: 'A rare example of conscientious and loving typography, and what for want of a better word we must call palaeolatry.'

It is strange that sufferers concentrate on the lost glories of the past, forgetting slavery, child labour and biannual baths if you were lucky.

Compare and contrast with 'mumpsimus', somebody who adheres to old ways in spite of the evidence that they are wrong; a bigoted opponent of reform. This is an allusion to the story (in Richard Pace, *De Fructu*, 1517) of an English priest who, when corrected for reading 'quod in ore sumpsimus' in the Mass, replied, 'I will not change my old mumpsimus for your new sumpsimus.'

As in: 'You are a mumpsimus lost in palaeolatry, Michael, to suppose that life was better before the war.'

PATHOPOEIA

A speech or figure of speech designed to arouse feelings: anger, grief, passion. For example, Henry V's speeches before the Battle of Agincourt. Rhyme with 'Pass the beer'. Adapted from the Greek for 'passion-making'. A term of rhetoric.

Phillips, *The New World of English Words*, 1678: 'Pathopoeia, an Expression of a Passion, in Rhetorick it is a figure by which the mind is moved to hatred, anger or pity.'

Other examples are Munch's 'The Scream'; the riot at the Abbey Theatre, Dublin, in 1907, at the opening of Synge's *The Playboy of the Western World* (did Synge mean to provoke anger?); and the first movement of Stravinsky's *The Rite of Spring*, which provoked a riot at its first performance in Paris in 1913.

As in: 'Don't scream, Emily. I am impervious to your pathopoeia.'

PAVONISE

To peacock. To comport oneself as a peacock might do. To show off. To strut and flaunt one's virtual feathers in a vain fashion. To do the human equivalent of scratching and pecking the ground in the hope of finding grains of food, to spread one's tail feathers and to clean one's hindquarters with one's mouth. Rhymes (extravagantly) with 'Salmon eyes'.

The word comes – like two thirds of the language – from the Latin, *pavo*, a peacock. Hence Florio (the seventeenth-century English lexicographer) introduced into his Italian glossary *pavoneggiare*, to peacockise it.

'Pavonine' means of or pertaining to, resembling or characteristic of, a peacock. 'Pavonious' means ocellated (having little eyes) like a peacock's tail.

Thackeray, *The Book of Snobs*, 1848: 'The lanky pavonine strut, and shrill genteel scream.'

Ruskin, *The Stones of Venice*, 1851: 'Groups of peacocks and lions not expressive of very accurate knowledge either of leonine or pavonine forms.'

A kinder word with which to educate small girls than 'showing-off'.

As in: 'We all admire your red shoes, Rosalind, but that is probably enough pavonising in front of the rest of the class.'

PECCABILITY

Capable of sinning. An adaptation of the medieval Latin *peccabilis*. Classical Latin *peccare* is to sin, with different connotations before the Christian fathers got hold of the word.

John Donne (who else?), *Six Sermons*, 1631: 'The peccability, that possibility of sinning, which is in the nature of the angels of heaven.'

It is symptomatic of peccant human nature that 'impeccable' (not liable to sin), which seldom occurs in life rather than language, should so exceed in common use the word that connotes its converse. You might say that our lexicon is rich with words for imperfection, but no harm in bringing back the old word for a condition that is common to us all.

As in: 'A pedant might argue that there is peccability in your batting, Hugo, when you try to sweep the fast bowler over mid-wicket in his first over.'

PERIAPT

Something worn about the person as a charm. An amulet or bracelet. Adapted from the Greek by way of French in the sixteenth century.

Shakespeare, *King Henry VI*, 1591: (La Pucelle [Joan of Arc], the Wicked Witch, speaks): 'The Regent conquers and the Frenchmen fly, / Now help, ye charming spells and periapts...'

It sounds more expensive than bracelet and necklace, and carries old intimations of enchantment and antidote.

Coleridge, Lay Sermons, 1816: 'Superstition goes wandering with its pack of amulets, bead-rolls, periapts and fetishes.'

As in: 'Allow me to fasten this periapt around your neck, Natasha; it will last longer than a Gerald Ratner prawn sandwich.'

PERISTERONIC

Pertaining to or concerned with pigeons. Evidently from the Greek *peristeron*, a dovecote, *peristera*, a dove or pigeon.

You might protest that the uses of this forgotten word are limited, but we are a nation of pigeon fanciers and racers of pigeons.

Fulton and Wright, *The Book of Pigeons*, 1876: 'Who would talk of a pigeon's "eyelids" that has any knowledge of matters peristeronic?'

And, metaphorically, Joanna Cannan, *High Table*, 1931: 'A discourse which Anne and Cecilia punctuated with polite little peristeronic sounds.'

There is glory for you in the ocean of English to know a word meaning 'suggestive of pigeons', used not for showing off, but for the delight of feathered things.

As in: 'Trafalgar Square has become less peristeronic since they banned the sellers of nuts and other pigeon fodder.'

PERPOTATION

Drinking. Rhyme, approximately, with 'her rotation'. Adaptation of the rare Latin *perpotatio*, continued drinking; a drinking bout. The prefix *per* normally means 'through', 'by means of'. It does not usually mean 'excessive' per se and per saltum, so this meaning must be per accidens.

There are so few citations in Latin that we have to deduce the meaning. The rare citations of this lost word in English do not help.

Henry Cockeram defined the word in 1623 as 'ordinarie drunkennesse'. Nathan Bailey defined the same word in 1721 as 'a thorough drunkenness'. Was Cockeram a lush? Or was Bailey a prude who could not hold his liquor? They are past our adjudication, but we have room for an elegant lost word for the English vice that still fouls our streets at weekends.

As in: 'Could I risk a small, very dry fino, Joseph, without being accused of indulging in perpotation?'

PETARD

A bomb or mine. A small engine of war used to blow in a door, to make a breach in a wall, to break down drawbridges. Originally of metal; later a wooden box, charged with powder and fired by a fuse.

For those who know their Onions (the Shakespearean commentator), *Hamlet*, 1604: 'For 'tis the sport to have the engineer / Hoist with his own petar(d): and it shall go hard / But I will delve one yard below their mines, / And blow them at the moon.'

Petard can be used figuratively. Butler, *Hudibras*, 1678: '... eternal Noise and Scolding. The Conjugal Petard, that tears Down all Portcullises of Ears.'

It can also be used as a verb. Carlyle, *The French Revolution*, 1837: 'A wicker Figure is promenaded, then solemnly consumed by fire, with such petarding and huzzaing.'

The little bomb comes from the French verb *peter*, to break wind or fart. Le Pétomane (Joseph Pujol) used to entertain the audience at the Moulin Rouge with musical farting.

Our lexicon has room for an elegant word for an inelegant but universal bodily function.

As in: 'That was a petard you let off in your article, Ebenezer.'

PETECURE

No. Nothing to do with corns, bunions or toenails. 'Petecure' rhymes, just about, with 'Pedicure'. But it means 'small cookery', the kind that most of us do: baked beans on toast rather than *oeufs pochés au Grand Duc de Bourgogne*. Anglo-French from the Old French *petite Keuerie*. Cf. Petty Cury, the name of a street in Cambridge.

Liber Cocorum, c. 1420: 'Of petecure I will preach / What falls for you to know will I teach.'

Very few of us eat in an epicurean fashion, like vulgar Trimalchio or, better, Lucullus; but most of us understand 'epicurean'. Epicurus was an Athenian philosopher (c. 300 BC) who held that the highest good is pleasure, which he identified with the practice of virtue, not fine dining. He also believed that the gods do not concern themselves with dinner or other mortal affairs. A great many people eat scrambled eggs in a simple fashion, but nobody knows the word for this. Odd.

We have room in the kitchen for this lost word to describe what most of us get up to in there.

As in: 'Brace yourselves, my dears: I am in the kitchen, so it is petecure night.'

PETRICHOR

A pleasant, distinctive smell that often accompanies the first rain after a long period of warm, dry weather in certain regions. Derived from *petra*, the Greek for a rock, with *ichor*, in mythology the ethereal juice in the veins of the gods.

Bear & Thomas, *Nature*, 1964: 'The diverse nature of the host materials has led us to propose the name "petrichor" for this apparently unique odour ... This name, unlike the general term "argillaceous odour", avoids the ... implication that the phenomenon is restricted to clay or argillaceous materials; it does not imply that petrichor is necessarily a fixed chemical entity but rather it denotes an integral odour.'

In this soggy land occasions to use this word will be rare, but what delight to have a word to fix the smell of rain on dry ground. A jolly sight better than argillaceous odour, non?

As in: 'Breathe in deeply, Lillian, and enjoy the petrichor – this is a rare opportunity.'

PHILODOX

Properly (etymologically, from the ancient Greek), somebody who loves fame or glory. But taken erroneously (after 'orthodox') as one who loves his own opinion: an argumentative or dogmatic person. Plato coined the word to mean 'lover of opinion'. Rhymes (approximately) with 'Kill a fox'.

Montaigne, *Essays*, trans. John Florio, 1603: 'No people are less Philosophers than Plato's Philodoxes, or lovers of their own opinions.'

Plato, *The Republic*, trans. J. L. Davies and D. J. Vaughan, 1852: 'Philodoxical rather than philosophical, that is to say, lovers of opinion rather than lovers of wisdom.'

In the tough and fumble of public affairs, it is a pity that the adjective is applicable to so many who have never heard of Plato or Montaigne.

Don't be irritatingly philodox, Phil.

As in: 'Does it not strike you, Larry, that the presenters of the *Today* programme are a touch philodox?'

PIGSNEY

Or 'pigsny', 'pigsnie', et al.: 'darling'. Somebody specially cherished; a pet; commonly used as an endearing form of address, chiefly applied to a woman or a girl. From the Saxon word for a female person. Literally 'pig's eye', taken as a familiar type of a small eye. 'Bird's-nie' and 'pinkeny' (tiny eye) followed the same route as terms of endearment, and are found passim in English literature.

Chaucer, *The Miller's Tale*: 'She was a prymerole, a pigsney for any lord to leggen in his bed.'

Robert Southey, *The Doctor* (which first published *The Story of the Three Bears*, the classic children's Goldilocks story), 1834: 'When pigsnie arrives and the purchaser opens the close sedan chair in which she has been conveyed to his house.'

English is not short of terms of endearment, but this is a curious old literary one. Try it on your inamorata. She will surely be charmed and flattered?

As in: 'Come, Jacqueline, my little pigsney: what would you like for supper?'

POPINJAY

A feather-headed and conceited young coxcomb. An earlier name for a parrot, found in *The Shipman's Tale* by Chaucer. The medieval Greek and Arabic forms probably represent the imitation of the cry of the bird in some African or other language from another Parrot-Land. The ending appears to have arisen by assimilation to the name of the European chattering bird, the jay.

In its evolution 'popinjay' came to mean the figure of a parrot on a pole as a mark to shoot at. But who on Earth first had the notion of using a parrot as a target? How was the parrot fastened to the pole? What did the parrot think of it? What, above all, was it a target for?

Well, I can answer one of these vexing questions. They have been shooting at poor Poll with crossbows, longbows and 'Peeces' since the sixteenth century.

1548: 'I saw on a Sunday this Lent strangers shooting at ye popinjay with crossbows.'

The popinjay is also used as an heraldic charge or bearings; also as the sign of an inn.

As in: 'Let me lend you my Pop weskit, George, to make you a veritable popinjay.'

POSTFERMENT

Removal to an inferior office (post or job, not word factory); the opposite of 'preferment'. Rhyme with 'Roast serpent'. Adapted by analogy from the Latin *praeferre*, to put before or forward. It is close in meaning to demotion, but it has a broader connotation.

Thomas Fuller, *Worthies of England*, 1662: 'Alexander Nevil, Arch-Bishop of York, was translated to St Andrews. This translation was a Post-Ferment, seeing the Arch-Bishoprick of St Andrews was subjected in that age unto York.'

The action is unusual in our age of human rights and respect for all. The management needs to present postferment as promotion.

As in: 'Dear Boy, look not upon your removal from darts and draughts editor to general reporter as postferment.'

PROCACITY

Forwardness and petulance. Sauciness or pertness. Unattractive cheek. Latin *procax*, forward or bold; hence, *procacitas*, impudence. Pronounce to rhyme, broadly and bankerly, with 'Pro the City'.

Not to be confused with precocity. 'I think that your Molly shows considerable procacity,' you say to Lady Pushmepullieux, when her daughter has just beaten your Isabel for the part of Dorothy in the end-of-term production of *The Wizard of Oz*.

Bishop Richard Mo(u)ntague, *Diatribae*, 1621: 'Let Scaliger pay for his malapert procacity against Paulus, concerning ignorance.'

Procacity has pupped no adjective in English. But the noun is a useful forgotten word, weightier than pertness or petulance.

This is a grown-up word for use in reviewing with the intention of giving offence. Should reviewers ever have this intent? Discuss. No.

As in: 'I prefer the suavity of Horace and Saint Matthew to the procacity and precocity of Martial and Saint Paul.'

PROLEGOMENON

A posh intro. A preliminary discourse prefixed to a literary work. Especially: a learned preface or preamble. Chiefly in the plural, 'prolegomena', introductory or preliminary observations on the subject of a book. Greek for 'things said beforehand'. An impressive substitute for preface or prologue.

Walter Scott, *Heart of Midlothian*, intro to the reader: 'Therefore have I chosen, in this prolegomenon, to unload my burden of thanks at thy feet.'

Charles Kingsley, letter to F. D. Maurice, 1869: 'They are meant as prolegomena to natural theology.'

The principal faults, as in most scribbling and speaking, are prolixity and verbosity. Cut the prolegomena and get to the matter in hand. Like good canapés, good prolegomena whet the appetite for the main course without exhausting or satiating the feeder/reader.

As in: 'I humbly [!] offer this edition with notes Variorum and the Prolegomena of Scriblerus Anon.'

QUAKEBUTTOCK

A humorously scathing word for a coward. Quake is derived from the Old English stem group, *cwac-*, implying instability. Buttock is a derivative of 'butt', meaning the thicker end of an instrument.

To note the connection between cowardice and weaponry is counterintuitive.

Beaumont and Fletcher, *Wit at Several Weapons*, 1616: 'Stand putting in one foot, and shiver ... like a quake-buttock.'

There are several synonyms for a coward in the English language, such as poltroon, invertebrate and milksop, but what English lacks is a word that is at once witty and emotive.

Note other cognate forms with *cwac-* in quake-belly, denoting a person with a trembling paunch, and quakemire, a Middle English precursor to quagmire, meaning a soft, trembling bog.

Richard Stanyhurst, 'Description of Ireland' in Holinshed's *Chronicles*, 1807: 'He was forced to fasten the quakemire with hurdle, and upon them to build the city.'

As in: 'I knew that you would never jump, Peter: You always were a dreadful quakebuttock.'

QUARESIMAL

To describe a meal: unsatisfying, meagre, austere, skimpy, having the qualities of inadequate (fasting, hungry) grub. Rhyme (drunkenly) with 'Where is the Kummel?' Adaptation of the Italian word for Lenten.

James Joyce, letter, 1923: 'Can we not have a quaresimal dinner somewhere together?'

Joyce supplies the only citation in the *OED*. He coined many other words: impotentising (describing something that makes one impotent); pelurious (hairy); and smellsip (to smell and sip at the same time).

In general, it is bad manners (showing off) to use obscure hendecasyllabic words. However, it is prudent to assume that readers of this book possess huge vocabs and are interested in language. For everyday purposes, go for Lenten.

Rosencranz: 'To think, my lord, if you delight not in man, what Lenten entertainment the players shall receive from you.'

But for wordplay among friends, I quite fancy 'quaresimal'. Logophiliac and civilised.

As in: 'I congratulate you, dear Marianne, on a quaresimal feast.'

RAPIN

In the UK, an (unruly) arts student. Contrariwise, in France, an apprentice in an artist's studio. The French eponym.

M. S. van de Velde's translation of H. Lavedan's *Mamzelle Vertu* in *French Fiction of Today*, 1891: 'Nothing disturbed her, neither the stifled laughter of a group of rapins in front of a Hercules, or the "shocking" bleated by a herd of English female visitors.'

Gerald du Maurier, *Trilby*, 1894: 'From the kind of laughter with which the points were received by the rapins in Carrel's studio he guessed these little songs were vile.'

You may not meet many arts students in your daily round, but if you should bump into one, this is the perfect word to describe him/her and make her/him believe that it is not intended as an insult. A genuine rapin would take it as a compliment.

As in: 'Of course you may bring your friend from arts class to supper, Lucinda, but I do hope that she is not a rapin.'

RECRUDESCENCE

Breaking out again. Of a quality or state of things (usually bad), for instance a disease or epidemic, or a wound or sore. From the Latin *recrudescere*: to become raw or crude again. Rhyme, approximately, with 'Eh, rude essence?'

Its usage to mean the resurgence of something good is castigated in *The King's English*, 1908, by the Fowler bros: 'Recrudescence is becoming quite a fashionable journalistic word. It properly means the renewed inflammation of a wound ... to use it of persons or their histories is absurd.'

It is used in the original 'boo' sense by John Stuart Mill in *Auguste Comte and Positivism*, 1865: 'The recrudescence of a metaphysical Paganism in the Alexandrian schools.'

There is worthy work for a flavoured word instead of the bland, non-commital 'reappearance'. I vote for a recrudescence of this word.

As in: 'I do not want a recrudescence of this ancient sibling jealousy, boys.'

REDELESS

Not knowing what to do in an emergency. Devoid or destitute of counsel. Rhyme with 'Read less!' (rotten advice).

Rede (counsel or advice given by one person to another) is a common Teutonic word, very frequent in Old English and early Middle English. It remained in literary use until the beginning of the seventeenth century. After that date it is rarely found until revived in archaic and poetic diction in the nineteenth century.

The Rev. John Richard Green, *The Conquest of England*, 1883: 'The opponents of Eadward dreaded that he would be what they afterwards called Aethelred – a king "redeless" or uncounselled.'

Ethelred the Unready.

Flapping like a headless chicken in an emergency is a common fault. Rum that 'savoir faire', knowing what to do in an emergency (a much rarer quality), has survived and thrives, while its converse has faded away.

As in: 'Don't be so recklessly redeless, Edward: for once listen to my advice.'

REMORD

This is a protean word of many shades of meaning, including: to afflict a person with painful feelings; to remember with regret; to feel or awaken remorse; to ponder. It comes from the Latin *remordere*, to bite back, sting or attack. Rhyme, almost, with 'reward'.

Charles Reade, *White Lies*, 1857: 'Others thought he must at some part of his career have pillaged a church ... and now was committing the mistake of remording himself about it.'

Sir William Mure, *True Crucifixe*, 1629: 'Yet from his lips not one intemperate word / His merciless tormentors doth remord.'

We have no single word that expresses 'to feel remorse'. Repent, regret and rue don't quite do it. As a noun, remord as a touch of remorse sounds a bit like a drop of milk being added to your coffee. But as a verb it renders poetic any decision made and subsequently regretted, such as the choice you made not to chat up that young woman on the train to Brighton, or the choice you made last night to drink the third Scotch.

As in: 'I cannot help remording that I did not pay more attention during my German classes at school.'

REPERTITIOUS

Meaning found by chance. Rhymes, roughly, with 'Superstitious'. Adaptation of the Latin *repertitius*, from *reperire*, to find.

Repertitious has not had as much success in entering the lexicon as its almost-synonym, serendipitous. This is probably because it has not had so influential a sponsor.

Horace Walpole invented serendipitous from Serendip, the former name of Ceylon and then Sri Lanka. In a letter of 28 January 1754, Walpole writes that he had coined it after the title of his fairytale, *The Three Princes of Serendip*, the heroes of which 'were always making discoveries, by accidents and sagacity, of things they were not in quest of'.

Repertitious is a century older, being recorded in Thomas Blount's 1656 dictionary. But it does not have the fairytale charm of serendipitous; and it is madly confusable with repetitious.

Thus the score: Authors 1 – Lexicographers 0. Do we need so close a synonym? No. But there is no harm in having a precise alternative tool in your word-bag.

As in: 'To meet you at the Wigmore Hall is not entirely repertitious, my dear.'

RODOMONTADE

A boastful or bragging speech. Hence, boastful or bragging words or behaviour. This is the eponym of the boastful Saracen leader in Ariosto's *Orlando Furioso* (1516), an epic poem that was immensely popular. Stress on the fourth syllable, di-di-didum, to rhyme, just about, *mutatis mutandis*, with 'O God, you're HARD'.

Thomas Macaulay, *The History of England*, 1849: 'Wherever he came he pressed horses in defiance of law, and almost raised mobs by his insolent rodomontades.'

Generalised, William Hazlitt, *Table-Talk*, 1822: 'A profusion of barbarous epithets and wilful rhodomontade [sic].'

As a word it can mean a braggart or boaster (also 'rodomont').

John Aubrey, *Brief Lives*, 1697: 'There was a Rhadamontade [sic] that would fight with any man and bragged of his valour.'

Boasting and bragging is deemed bad form in polite English society, but there is still plenty of it around: note the rodomontades of a base football player when he has scored a goal.

This is a useful literary putdown for silly swanking.

As in: 'Speak softly, Oscar, and carry your rodomontade in reserve.'

ROORBACK

A false report or slander invented for political purposes.

James K. Polk was the eleventh President of the United States (1845–49). The pocket Napoleon of the stump, he was, according to the historian Paul F. Boller, 'totally lacking personal magnetism or even quiet charm'. During the campaign for the presidency, a forgery slandering Polk was published, purporting to be taken from *The Travels of Baron Roorback*.

H. L. Mencken: 'Since the exposure of the fraud actually helped Polk, the word is sometimes spelled roarback.'

This old word is useful for describing the propaganda aired in all party political broadcasts.

As in: 'It cannot in the opinion of Her Majesty's Government be described as a stealth tax without some risk of being classified as a roorback.'

RUFFING

The action of applauding by stamping one's feet, rather than clapping one's hands. Rhyme with 'puffing', 'stuffing' and (in posh accent) 'muffin'.

Said by the *OED* to be derived from 'to ruff' (not Bridge, you fool), to beat a 'ruff' or ruffle upon (a drum). Also, intransitive (of a drum) to be thus beaten.

Better than 'ruff' in falconry, 'to strike (the quarry) without securing it'. I doubt this derivation. Pull the other talon, it's got bells on.

Thomas Carlyle, *Froude*, 1843: 'Ruffing of applausive barristers over table oratory heard at a distance.'

This is a donnish form of applause, suited to lecture halls and livery company dinners (where the audience is too full to rise to a standing ovation) rather than party conferences. It is a brilliant word that refills a hole in the language. 'Stamping one's feet in applause' does not carry the same brevity and onomatopoeia.

As in: 'You may now applaud the Head: may I suggest some dignified ruffing?'

SARDANAPALIAN

Camp and OTT. Luxuriously effeminate.

The eponym of Sardanapalus, the last King of Nineveh, also known as Ashurbanipal. (He was the last of the great Assyrian kings and his reign, 668–627 BC, marks the zenith of Assyrian splendour.) His name is also used for a legendary king who was supposed to have lived in outrageous luxury. After being besieged by the Medes for two years, a concubine persuaded Sardanapalus to place himself on a funeral pyre. She set fire to it and the inferno consumed him, her, the palace and entire court. The legend of this Sardanapalus cannot be connected with the historic Sardanapalus (or any Assyrian king known through archaeology). So he is probably a xenophobic Greek legend. Pronounce roughly to rhyme with 'Guard a nap, Alien'.

Andrew Marvell, *The Rehearsal Transpros'd*, 1673: 'You muster up all Christian Princes to Neronize and Caligulize them, unless they will chuse to be Uilenspiegled and Sardanapalized by you.'

As in: 'Piers, your cooking and hospitality are positively Sardanapalian.'

SARDONIAN

Somebody who flatters with deadly intent.

This word occurs first in Homer, but its etymology is obscure. It is the descriptive epithet for bitter or scornful laughter. Roman pedants changed Homer's spelling to imply that it has primary reference to the effects of eating a Sardinian plant (Latin: *herba Sardonia*), which was said to cause facial convulsions resembling horrible laughter, usually before death.

Bishop Barlow, *Answering Nameless Catholics*, 1609: 'His nature is too noble to be a Sardonian: Fawning and Crouching he leaves to such base bone-gnawers as Father Parsons.'

Rude.

As in: 'Thank you for your effusive herogram: I hope that it is not Sardonian.'

SARVODAYA

This word, generally forgotten, means 'the well-being [or prosperity] of all'. Deployed by Gandhi (1869–1948) to mean a new social order without caste, based on non-violence and service. Sanskrit *sarva* means 'all'; *udaya* means 'uplift, prosperity'. Rhyme, roughly and non-violently, with 'Halve a buyer'.

Bombay Chronicle, 1919: 'The committee has selected the following prohibited books for dissemination – *Sarvodaya* by M. K. Gandhi.'

Harijan, 1948: 'Samaj, which corresponds more to brotherhood than to association. The Sarvodaya Samaj has been established to strive towards a society based on Truth and Non-violence, in which there will be no distinction of caste or creed.'

Gandhi's Utopian society of friends is a consummation devoutly to be wished. Has there ever been a classless and creedless society of brothers and sisters? Oops, remember Cain and Abel. One day we will get there. Please don't say, 'And pigs will fly.'

As in: 'Now Peregrine, we are going to play a game called Sarvodaya, or Saki's The Toys of Peace.'

SCROUGE

To incommode by pressing against (a person); to encroach on (a person's) space in sitting or standing. To crowd. Also, to push or squeeze (a thing). Apparently an onomatopoeic alteration of 'scruze', to screw or squeeze.

Dickens, *The Old Curiosity Shop*, 1840: 'Kit had hit a man on the head with a handkerchief of apples for scrouging his parent with unnecessary violence.'

Anybody who travels on public transport experiences the squashing denotation of this word every day. One wishes that one did not need it so often.

As in: 'No need to scrouge me, Sir. There is plenty of room at the end of the carriage.'

SHOTCLOG

An unwelcome companion tolerated because he pays the shot for the rest. A 'shot' is the charge, amount due or to be paid, especially at a tavern or for entertainment; or one's share in such entertainment. A 'clog' is a useful lump or block.

Ben Jonson, *Every Man Out of His Humour*, 1599: 'If you be out [of humour] keep your distance, and be not made a Shotclog no more.'

A most unpopular character among the Hooray Henry boozing classes is somebody slow to pay when it is his round. English is rich in words for the mean: tightwad, skinflint, lickpenny ... but none of them has the geographical connotation that the curmudgeonly codger, as burr-like as Horace's Pest, is in the pub, reaching too slowly for his money when it is his round.

As in: 'Don't be such a shotclog, Percy: mine's a treble Scotch.'

SKIRR

A sound of a whirring, grating or rasping character. Onomatopoeic. Useful for twitchers and other bird-watchers. Possibly from the Latin *excurrere*, to run hastily (away), by way of the Old French *escorre*, but I shouldn't bet your Barbour on it.

Hardy, *Far from the Madding Crowd*, 1874: 'The skirr of whetting [sc. shears] spread into the sky.'

Hardy, *Woodlanders*, 1887: 'The occasional skirr of a halter in Melbury's stables.'

Hardy's continual use of the word suggests that it is West Country dialect, as well as descriptive and echoic.

Both easier to say and more vivid than 'whirr'.

As in: 'Listen to the skirr of pigeons, those London unemployables in shabby grey suits.'

SOLIPSIST

One who believes that only she/he her/himself is real, and that the external world exists only through her/his own conception of it. From the Latin *solus*, alone, plus *ipse*, self.

The Contemporary Review, 1884: 'As long as we confine ourselves to the world given in experience we must profess solipsism.'

The word will do for any extremely self-centred person. For example, somebody who drives with his windows open and the radio blaring, or who arrives at the top of the escalator in a very crowded Westfield, stands stock still and looks about in a leisurely fashion. Solipsists, the lot of them.

Boswell observed of Bishop Berkeley's material-solipsistic theory of the non-existence of matter that, though they were satisfied it was not true, they were unable to refute it. Johnson struck his foot against a large stone, exclaiming: 'I refute it thus.' It is sport to imagine two philosophers at a seminar eyeing each other and wondering which of them really exists.

Good posh word for somebody extremely selfish.

As in: 'When it comes to choosing which television programme to play, you are a solipsist, Martin.'

SPHRAGISTICS

The study or knowledge of seals or signet rings. *Sphragis* is Greek for a seal. Ancient Greeks named the Egyptian priest who kept the temple seal *Sphragistes*.

Partington, 1836: 'Sphragistics is a branch of diplomatics which teaches the history of seals and the means [to determine] the genuineness of the documents to which they are attached.'

You might retort that this is a lost word so esoteric that it is scarcely worth reviving. But no word is utterly useless. And not just for swanking casual references to one's recondite pursuits and studies: 'I remember, back in the days when I was reading sphragistics at Trinity ...' You may feel qualms about this pursuit. The study seems harmless enough, but the cruelty of the actual engraving process on those harmless marine creatures...

This is a useful minor word for those interested in art, archaeology and museums. Could it be transferred metaphorically?

As in: 'I applaud your passion for carving, Neville, but I would rather you did not practise sphragistics on the kitchen table.'

STEATOPYGOUS

Having a big bum. Fat-buttocked. Pertaining to or characterised by 'steatopyga': a protruberance of the buttocks due to an abnormal accumulation of fat in and behind the hips and thighs, found as a racial characteristic of certain peoples, especially the Hottentot Bushmen of South Africa; and, we might add, increasingly among the overfed classes of the United States and the United Kingdom.

Greek *stear-*, *steat-* means 'fat'; *pugee* is the rump or buttocks. The Rudston Venus mosaic from a Roman villa in Yorkshire shows Venus with small breasts and a big bottom tapering to tiny feet. Is this the ideal of beauty in a cold northern climate? Yes.

An excellent obscure word for insulting without offending. To make personal remarks about other bottoms invites an obvious retort. But with the way civilisation is growing in congestion for seats in aeroplanes and cinemas, we are going to have an increasing use for 'steatopygous' and related words.

As in: 'A Mars a day makes you fit, fast and steatopygous, Jessica.'

SUBTRIST

Somewhat sad. A bit low. Rhyme (roughly) with 'club fist'.

Sir Walter Scott (that logophile resurrection man of lost words), *The Abbot*, 1820: 'You look subtrist and melancholic.'

You might argue that we have plenty of words to express this notion: melancholy, blue, glum, sad, forlorn, down in the mouth, gloomy and so on, from doleful to lachrymose. But the Romance languages have *triste*, and English is the gannet of words and takes them wherever it likes the sound of them.

So, Wot the Tartarus. Subtrist has a fine, forlorn, frowning French resonance. Go for it.

As in: 'Nobody loves me; everybody hates me; I'm going to the garden to eat worms.' 'Cheer up, Lucian; to be subtrist is human, but it does not help.'

SUCCEDANEUM

A posh substitute. A thing that (rarely, a person who) replaces or serves in the place of another. Rhyme, (very) roughly, with 'Suck 'n' see uranium'. Oh, forget it.

Horace Walpole, letter, 1774: 'In lieu of me, you will have a charming succedaneum.'

Dickens, Dombey, 1848: 'A pair of dreadnought pilot-trousers, whereof the waistband was so very broad and high that it became a succedaneum for a waistcoat.'

Why do we need such a Latinate word when we are familiar with the common sub, from the foot-ballers' bench? Well, there are contexts, usually scholarly, when 'succedaneum' is more appropriate without being pompous.

'Substitute' implies second best. Succedaneum is a successor, with no implication of inferiority. English is rich in such words: surrogate, proxy, ersatz; succedaneum claims its particular niche.

As in: 'Since you have parents' evening, Oliver, I am happy to act as your succedaneum for the late shift.'

SUMPTUARY

Pertaining to or regulating expenditure. Making the pay packet last the week. The epithet with which Wilkins Micawber was in love, but had trouble managing. Adapted from the Latin *sumptus*, *suptuarius*, expenditure, to do with expenditure.

In medieval history, a sumptuary law regulated expenditure, especially with a view to restraining excess in food, dress etc., to stop the plebs from rivalling their national patricians and superiors.

Nathaniel Hawthorne, *The Scarlet Letter*, 1850: 'Of a splendour beyond what was allowed by the sumptuary regulations of the colony.'

Try not to confuse with sumptuous, costly, splendid, which comes from the same root.

Milton, *Paradise Lost*, 1671: 'Sumptuous gluttonies and gorgeous feasts.'

As the organ thunders Wagner, and Joanna and Jocelyn proceed down the aisle, you whisper, 'Ah. The sumptuary getting hitched to the sumptuous.'

As in: 'I simply cannot afford another pair of red shoes, Amy; we must have some sumptuary prudence in this household.'

SUPERCHERY

An attack made upon someone who is at a disadvantage; (a piece of) foul play. Derived, by way of Italian and French, from the popular Latin *superculus*, where *super* means OTT. Rhyme, very approximately, with 'You berk, Mary'.

The Earl of Monmouth, translating Boccalini's *Advertisements from Parnassus*, 1656: '[The] swaggering companions, which he was accustomed to make use of in his supercheries and foul play to men of honour.' Hence, the word came to mean trickery and deceit.

Horace Walpole, in a letter to Horace Mann, the British Minister to the court of Tuscany, 1781: 'That I might not contribute to any legal supercherie[y], I insisted [etc.] ...' A cheap (though useful) word for a cheap act.

Compare with 'barla-fumble' – in sport or play, a call for a pause or truce from one who is at a disadvantage. The modern schoolyard cries for seeking a truce are 'time out' and 'uncle' (American). It is bad enough to admit defeat without having to use a word that sounds as silly as 'barla-fumble'.

As in: 'It was a superchery to test me on the 7-times table without warning, Millicent.'

SUPERFIDEL

Believing too much; overly credulous. Contrary to what you might reasonably suppose, 'SuperFidel' does not refer to a cigar-smoking communist superhero from Cuba, though it could reasonably be applied to his remaining fans. Adaptation of the Latin *super*, in its sense of OTT, plus *fidelis*, trusting, credulous. Rhyme, arduously, with 'Glue the fiddle'. An extension of 'semifidel', derived, with difficulty, from 'infidel'.

Robert Southey, *The Doctor* (a miscellany of anecdotes, quotation and comment), 1834: 'Some of the infidel, some of the semifidel, and some of the superfidel schools.'

In our age of enthusiastic credulity about every absurdity, this is a dry lost word worth resurrection. And bring back 'gobemouche', the French for somebody who credulously accepts all news, however absurd. In French, *gobemouches* (somebody who swallows flies) is the form employed for both singular and plural. English writers treat the French form as plural and use gobemouche as the singular.

As in: 'You are superfidel to take me as your partner in the foursome, Lydia.'

SUPERVACANEOUS

No, not milking more cows than you can shake a stick at. This word is a self-referential example of itself. It is an OTT way of saying OTT, with a touch of verbal vanity thrown into the word-pot. It means 'vainly added over and above what is essential': superfluous, redundant. Derived from the Latin *super*, extra, plus *vacare*, to be empty or void, plus the stock ending for Latin translated into an English adverb, '-eous'.

Jeremy Bentham, *Official Aptitude Maximised*, 1825: 'Desire is sufficient: accomplishment, or anything like and approach to it, is supervacaneous.'

This is an agreeable put-down word for somebody whose garrulity or opinions seem to you OTT. He may take the 'super' for a compliment.

As in: 'Protests are supervacaneous, Alice: I insist that you have the last éclair.'

TACENDA

Shh. Whisht. Let's not go there. Things to be passed over in silence. Matters not to be mentioned. The unmentionable in pursuit of the embarrassing. Such as Aunt Rosie's first husband. Where that scar really came from. Who finished the chocolate biscuits? The gerundive neuter plural of the Latin verb *tacere*, to be silent. Rhyme, pushing it a bit, with 'Back tender'.

Thomas Carlyle, dear old logophile, *Past & Present*, 1843: 'Willelmus Sacrista, and his bibations and tacenda, are softly yet irrevocably put an end to.'

S. H. Hodgson, *Theory of Practice*, 1870: 'A greater number of things are classed among tacenda. The French term *pudeur* seems exactly to express the feeling which is called out painfully or wounded by an [sic] lifting of the veil of the tacenda.'

This learned but useful word overlaps, but does not replicate, the improper, the unmentionable, the discreditable and the shifty. Draw a Venn diagram of these similar but particular meanings, if you have otium. It fills a hole in the dam of modern English.

As in: 'Shall we consider your school reports for this term tacenda, Rupert?'

TAGHAIRM

To predict the future. To prognosticate. To prefabricate false fantasies.

Walter Scott (lovely tartan fogey antiquarian), *The Lady of the Lake*: 'To taghairm – a person was wrapped up in the skin of a newly slain bullock, and deposited beside a waterfall, or at the bottom of a precipice, or in some other strange, wild and unusual situation, where the scenery around him suggested nothing but objects of horror. In this situation he revolved in his mind the question proposed; and whatever was impressed upon him by his exalted imagination, passed for the inspiration of the disembodied spirits, who haunt these desolate recesses.'

Steady on, Philip. Surely this is an example of a useless word that has been lost precisely because nobody uses it any more, not even in the Scottish Highlands, where it was practised? But is it not worth reviving to put down pontificators, prophets, politicians, weather forecasters and other dodgy prophets who presume to predict our future?

As in: 'Jock, could you please taghairm the winner of the 4.30 at Musselburgh for me with your customary perspicacity?'

TERATISM

Love of the monstrous or prodigious. Greek *téras* means monster, a marvel or prodigy. Plural: *térata*. Pronounce to rhyme, roughly, with 'Firmer prism'.

'Teratosis' is a biological freak or monstrosity; a 'teratologist' deals in stories of marvels or prodigies, such as Herodotus; 'teratical' relates to monsters or marvels. Johnson defined 'teratology' as 'bombast, affectation of false sublimity'. But Uncle Sam was cribbing from Bailey's dictionary.

1722: 'Herodotus, possibly delighting in teratical stories.'

1856: 'The aimless fables and teratologies of Thomas the Israelite or the Gospels of the Infancy.'

After your sister and her boyfriend have spent half an hour on the phone, while you are desperate to use it, you may congratulate them on their mutual teratism, without exciting offence.

As in: 'Give me a blow-by-blow report of your match, Mortimer, omitting no details; I am in the mood for teratology.'

TRICHECHINE

An adjective meaning 'like a walrus (or manatee)'. Belonging or having the characteristics of the family *Trichechidae* or walruses. As a substantive, an animal of this family, a walrus. From the Greek for 'having hairs', hairy. 'Quia solus inter pisces fere hirsutus est' ('Because it is the only fish that is nearly hairy') – which is a category mistake as pleasant as the one that Alice made with her walrus.

Cf. Trichechodont, characterised by molar teeth like those of the manatee, with cusps confluent into two or more transverse crests. Hairy teeth? Don't let's go down that hole, as dark as a walrus's throat.

We seldom are lucky enough to meet manatees, or even walruses, on our daily round, except, perhaps, on holiday in the Western Isles. But this is a good adjective to describe a particular kind of unfortunate moustache, which one has the misfortune to encounter every day of the week.

As in: 'I know that modern fashion is extravagantly trichechine, Douglas. But you should tie your hair up if you do not want to give your opponents in the scrum a lever to pull on.'

TRIPUDIATE

To dance, skip, jump or leap for joy, or with excitement; to exult. Secondarily, to trample, stamp or jump (on or upon somebody) in contempt or triumph. Presumably from the Greek for '(with) three feet' (*tri poda*), and the Latin *tripudium*, a beating the ground with the feet, a leaping or dancing, a religious dance. The origin of the cha-cha-cha, perhaps?

From 1891: 'He will tripudiate upon the platform because his party have made a long legislative score.'

And second, from 1895: 'The people tore down the image, tripudiated on its shattered fragments.'

Skipping for joy might be considered undignified for adults. However, if the urge to skip overwhelms you, tripudiating makes the activity sound more dignified. In any case, who cares for dignity? And how can a tripod dance with three feet?

As in: 'They are playing our tune, Polly: would you care to tripudiate?'

TRUMPERY

Sam Johnson defines it as 'something of less value than it seems'. Such as your car. Worthless stuff, trash, rubbish. Adaptation of the Old French *tromperie*.

Washington Irving, *Salmagundi*, 1807: 'An abundance of trumpery and rubbish, with which the house is encumbered ... three-legged chairs, clocks without hands...'

Also applied to abstract things, as beliefs, practices, writing and so on. And, contemptuously, to religious practices, ceremonies, ornaments etc., regarded as idle or superstitious.

Joseph Pitts, 1704: 'They blame the Papists for having so many Trumperies in their Churches.'

We have plenty of such synonyms: rot, rubbish, amphigory ... But in our world of trumpery, celeb values and worship we can use another reminder of frailty of possessions that rolls around the tongue.

As in: 'Well, I will buy you the silver shoes, Catherine, though as an old bore I consider them trumpery.'

TURKISH

To transform, especially for the worse. To pervert.

Has this a racist implication? Probably not. The bulk of the first edition of the *Oxford English Dictionary* was compiled in the nineteenth and early twentieth centuries. So you would expect it to be filled with racist and otherwise offensive words. Not so. 'Frenchified' is listed, but without the sense given in other dictionaries: 'To be afflicted with a venereal disease.' Were the editors delicate? Improbable.

The derivation of Turkish is uncertain, but it is probably from the French *torquer*, an adaptation of the Latin *torquere*, to twist.

1607: 'Turkishing the story, or (to speak more properly) turning it into a mere fable.'

The word is more vigorous than its near-synonyms: twist, distort, pervert.

As in: 'The sub-editor has turkished my piece – as per bloody usual.'

ULTRACREPIDARIAN

An ignorant or presumptuous critic; one who ventures beyond his scope.

A cobbler criticised the way that Apelles of Colophon, the greatest artist of antiquity, had painted a shoe. Apelles replied, in Pliny's Latin translation: '*Sutor ne supra crepidam judicaret*' or 'A cobbler should not judge beyond the sole [of his shoes]' – or, in English idiom, 'Cobbler, stick to your last.'

William Hazlitt told William Gifford, the acerbic editor, in 1819: 'You have been well called an ultracrepidarian critic.'

As an adjective this useful word means going beyond one's proper province; giving opinions on matters beyond one's knowledge. Don't we all?

As in: 'Excuse my ultracrepidarianism, Rooney, but you should have passed the ball, not hoofed it over the bar.'

UTINAM

An earnest wish or fervent desire. Pronounce to rhyme (roughly) with 'Phew! This ham.' Adoption of the Latin for 'Oh that!', 'Would that!', 'I wish!'; the optative.

As in, Cicero, 'Ad Familiares': 'Quod utinam minus vitae cupidi fuissemus – Would that we had been less anxious for life.'

Sir Thomas Browne, that polysyllabic old quack, 'Religio Medici', 1643: ''Tis not a melancholy utinam of mine owne, but the desires of better heads.'

'The Entertainer', 1718: 'Our Religion is pure and undefiled ... A Glance or a Utinam, in Christianity, are Criminal.'

More wistful than desire, more elegant than longing, more intellectual than lust. Utinam is useful flotsam from the days when Latin was the world language and natural education for Europeans.

As in: 'You may have a utinam for ice cream, Melissa, but we were not sent into this world entirely for pleasure.'

<u>VECORDIOUS</u>

Obsessive, senseless, batty. From the Latin *vecors*, senseless, foolish; *vecordia*, folly. The lost English adjective's shorter form is 'vecord', the noun is 'vecordy'. Rhyme with (in the vile and vecord modern abbreviation) 'Records 'R' Us' or 'See swords on us'.

Swedenborg, *Wisdom of Angels*, translated 1788: 'Hence too the Terms Concord, Discord, Vecord (malicious Madness) and other similar Expressions.'

Interesting that this takes 'vecord' as a noun.

Blount, *Glossographia*, 1656: 'Vecordy, madness, trouble of mind, folly, doting.'

English is rich in words for, and references to, madness, e.g., the first clown in *Hamlet* on the plot to send Hamlet to England: 'Twill not be seen in him there. There the men are as mad as he.' So it would be economical to reserve 'vecordious' for obsessive rather than malicious folly, then it will be an elegant concealed insult for those whose enthusiasms we cannot share. Enthusiasm is usually vecordious as well as nasty.

As in: 'I shall be pleased to join in your cross-country treasure hunt, Mervyn. It is a vecordious activity.'

VELLEITY

A wish, desire, or inclination, without accompanying action or effort. Like the poor cat i' the adage (she loves fish, but fears to wet her paws). Adaptation of the Latin *velle*, to will or to wish.

T. S. Eliot, *Portrait of a Lady*, 1915: 'And so the conversation slips / Among velleities and carefully caught regrets / Through attenuated tones of violins / Mingled with remote cornets...'

Weaker than a wish, stronger than inertia.

As in: 'No, dearest, I am not being difficult; I always have a velleity for your mother to come to stay.'

<u>VENEFICIAL</u>

This can mean: (a) acting by poison, poisoning; (b) used in, or acting by, sorcery or witchcraft, as, for instance, in a witches' brew; (c) relating to the doings of Venus. Derived from *venenum*, Latin for poison, and/or Venus. Rhyme, approximately, with 'Men! Official!'

Sir Thomas Browne, *Pseudodoxia Epidemica*, (Vulgar Errors), 1646: 'As for the Magical Virtues in this plant, and conceived efficacy unto veneficial intentions, it seemeth unto me a Pagan relique derived from the ancient Druids.'

Browne again, *The Garden of Cyrus*, 1658: 'Why the Goddesses sit commonly cross-legged in ancient draughts, Since Juno is described in the same veneficial posture to hinder the birth of Hercules?'

Do we have poison, witches or Venus here? Here is a variant: 'The actual poison-ring of that veneficious bacchante, Lucretia Borgia.'

There will not be many occasions to revive this lost word, but the three meanings come together when you first cook a meal for your beloved.

As in: 'My darling, you will find the Borgia curried oysters veneficial.'

VICAMBULIST

Somebody who walks about in the streets; *vicus* is the Latin word for street, while *ambulare* means to walk.

The Etonian, 1822: 'To see and to be seen is the professed object of these unwearied vicambulists.'

Mortimer Collins, *Squire Silchester*, 1873: 'Many strangers were there among them, as Musical Willie, who vicambulated greatly, soon perceived.'

Now that 'streetwalker' has acquired a specialised and pejorative connotation, we need an old/new word to describe the sociable urban perambulation. Dickens and Gladstone vicambulated London by night. Mediterranean countries perambulate before dinner, to see and be seen.

As in: 'I know that you are a keen vicambulist, dear. But why do all your roads lead to the Rose and Crown?'

VIDENDA

Things worth seeing, or which deserve to be seen. Rhymes with 'Bin ender'. Construe it, pray: 'The neuter plural of the gerundive of the Latin *videre*, to see.' Bravo, Tom. Alpha Plus.

Laurence Sterne, *Tristram Shandy*, 1760: 'In my list, therefore, of videnda at Lyons, this, tho' last, – was not, you see, least.'

W. H. Auden, *Listener*, 1964: 'Windows averted from plausible videnda but admitting a light one could mend a watch by.'

These are the sights that guidebooks promise to tell you about but usually miss out, which is why you see guidebooks piled in heaps on barrows of unread, unreadable books at 5p a loss.

As usual with Latin, there is no single word in English other than this that conveys its meaning precisely. You are best to find out the videnda for yourself, with a like-minded friend. Observe how many words we take from *videre*, to see, Tom, and stick to your Latin. Viz (videlicet, namely, to wit, you may see); video (coined as a visual equivalent of 'audio'), video game, video nasty, videophone, videotape ... etc., ad videndum.

As in: 'Let us have a cappuccino by the Rialto, Portia, before we delight in the Carpaccios and other videnda.'

VILIPEND

To contemn or despise. To rate or regard as being of little value or consequence. To treat contemptuously or slightingly. From the Latin *vilis*, *vile* or worthless, plus *pendere*, to consider or esteem. Very common c. 1500–1660, in some cases indistinguishable from later sense: to speak of with disparagement or contempt; to represent as contemptible or worthless; to abuse or vilify. Pronounce, roughly, to rhyme with 'Silly spend!'

Walter Scott (again), *Waverley*, 1814: 'A youth devoid of petulant volatility, which is impatient of, or vilipends, the conversation of his seniors.'

Sense (2), Thackeray, *Vanity Fair*, 1848: 'Menacing the youth and vilipending the poor innocent girl as the basest and most artful of vixens.'

Agreed that the English lexicon has a rich store of words for looking down one's nose at, which is a foundation activity of the English class system, both upwards and downwards. But the Latinate verb sounds richer and more contemptuous than its near-synonyms for the unpleasant activity.

As in: 'Do not vilipend a fiver, Humphry, but be grateful for small tips.'

VOCABULARIAN

Somebody who gives much or undue attention to words. From the Latin *vox*, a voice, *vocabulum*, a word. Rhyme, roughly, with 'No cab, you hairy one'.

Pall Mall Gazette, 1899: 'He is not a vocabularian; he uses, as none but a poet can, the old poetic materials.'

The great vocabularian and lexicographer Samuel Johnson wrote: 'I am not so lost in lexicography as to forget that words are the daughters of earth, and that things are the sons of heaven. Language is only the instrument of science, and words are but the signs of ideas: [yet] I wish ... that the instrument might be less apt to decay, and that signs might be permanent, like the things which they denote.'

Dream on, Sam. Nevertheless, language is a defining characteristic of us humans. We should aim to be vocabularians without becoming spidered in the web of words.

As in: 'Come on, Victoria, let's do your "spellings". We shall make a vocabularian of you.'

ZOILUS

A censorious, malignant or envious critic. The eponym of Zoilus, a Greek critic and grammarian (fourth century BC) famous for his severe criticism of Homer. Rhyme with 'Spoil us'.

Folk etymology mistakenly connects his name with *zeelos*, zeal. This is held to account for the association of the notion of malignancy or envy with the word.

Coleridge, *Notes & Lectures*, 1834: 'How then comes it that not only single zoili, but whole nations have combined in unhesitating condemnation of our great dramatist?'

Augustine also disliked reading Homer, but he had the excuse of finding Greek difficult.

Critics beware. If you heave the old harpoon too enthusiastically, you may find your name linked to that of an old carping nitpicker.

As in: 'Do you not think, Jasper, that "the pits of utter hogwash" might be classified as zoilism without major risk of terminological inexactitude?'

ZUGZWANG

A technical term from chess. A position in which a player is obliged to move but cannot do so without disadvantage; the disagreeable obligation to make such a move. German *zug*, move, plus *zwang*, compulsion or obligation. Rhyme (very roughly, more assonance) with 'Bug swam'.

Harry Golombek, former Chess Correspondent of *The Times*, *Fifty Great Games of Modern Chess*, 1942: 'Black has now only a few pawn moves left after which he is in a complete Zugzwang.'

Odd that this description has not been extended metaphorically into life, where it is common. It has been occasionally.

Country Life, 1973: 'She is, to use a chess term, in complete zugzwang. She could only make six tricks for a penalty of 200.'

The step from chess to bridge is small, so let's hear it for bloody zugzwang without apology. It traps us all.

As in: 'Forgive me for mentioning it, Tarquin, but you have put us in a zugzwang.'

WORD WATCHING

Language is a true democracy. Everybody who speaks it has input to it. If enough of us go on using a word such as 'wicked' or 'nice' in a new way, that word acquires an onion skin of new meaning. Likewise, if we refamiliarise ourselves with our lost words and their meanings, we can reintroduce them to our daily vocabulary.

There are longer books (dashed few). There are books with less jerky plot-lines. But none pack the heavy artillery of the *Oxford English Dictionary*. Twenty volumes (and rising), 300,000-plus main entries, 2.5 million illustrative quotations – this is a book to stop a jumbo jet, not a door. It is the emperor of dictionaries. It records English from the Old English of our rude Anglo-Saxon forefathers down to the rude English of our new generations.

Now the great dictionary grows electronically, daily on the internet. You can criticise the *OED*, if you dare. It is prescriptive, describing certain usages as (shock, horror) erroneous. It is elitist, recording published authors and not spoken chitchat. But it is the best choice for desert island reading, an essential tool for writers and a publication of great charm as well as weight. Where else would you find 'fatidical', 'lant' and 'acnestis'?

To read it from cover to cover is (dare I say this?) a waste of time. And impossible. I do not believe that Ammon Shea read every single word without nodding off. How could I wade through the 60,000 words describing the 430 meanings of 'set'?

But to dip in and out of the *OED*, and to peruse this compendium of the choicest lost words, will prevent you from 'gauming' in polite company and instead leave you with a reputation as a charming 'colloquialist'.

Now is the time to become the 'opsimath' among your friends. Over the next 'bouffage' might I suggest challenging the group to a spot of word watching. Simply read out the lost word and its three possible definitions, then allow people time to guess. The answers to each set are overleaf.

SPLURGUNDY
a. Extravagance
b. Wine
c. A shrub

PAIOCKE
a. A peacock
b. A person from the same town
c. A Basque ball-game

DONGLE
a. A she-ass
b. Software protection
c. To waste time

INTAGLIO
a. Shell-shaped pasta
b. A cut figure
c. Machicolation

CUECA
a. A dance
b. A lizard
c. A straw hat

SPLURGUNDY (b)

A sparkling red wine from Australia. Australians, who have a taste for the beverage not widely shared in the rest of the world, used to call it 'sparkling burgundy', but following the 1993 EU trade agreement, the use of European regional names for Australian wines was phased out. So this unofficial blend was coined to take its place. 1998: 'Splurgundy may be a wine of merit, but there's no denying that it is also an acquired taste.'

PAIOCKE (a)

An obscure word in Shakespeare (*Hamlet* III, ii, 295), conjectured to mean peacock (possibly a misprint for pacock; possibly equals pea-jock).

DONGLE (b)

A software protection device that must be plugged into a computer to enable the protected software to be used on it. An invented word (perhaps subliminally suggested by 'toggle'). 1982: 'The word "dongle" has been appearing in many articles with reference to security systems to computer software.'

INTAGLIO (b)

A figure cut into any substance. A stone or gem in which the design is hollowed out – the opposite to cameo. A countersunk die. A method of printing in which the image area is sunk into the surface of the plate – opposite to relief. Latin *talea* means a cutting, layer.

CUECA (a)

A South American dance. American Spanish from *zamacueca*, a South American Indian song and dance. 1928: 'The cueca, like the tango, comes from South America. It is the national dance of Chili [sic].'

STARRULET
a. A little star
b. A stream
c. A baldric

BASSALIA
a. A siege engine
b. A dance
c. The deep sea

AN SICH
a. A sick-note
b. In addition
c. In itself

SYMPLOCE
a. Rhetorical repetition
b. A plough shaft
c. A village idiot

CUDDY
a. A lover
b. A horse
c. Toffee

STARRULET (a)
A little star. Irregular formation after annulet and rivulet. 1610: 'But why have you noted some with Asterisks or Starrulets?'

BASSALIA (c)
The region of the deep sea. Adaptation of the late Latin *bassus*, deep, plus reference to the Greeks *hals*, sea. 1885: 'On the Ichthyological Peculiarities of the Bassalian Realm.'

AN SICH (c)
In itself. In the abstract. Not in relation to anything else. Originally taken from German philosophy. 1956: 'Much more widespread than the love of truth is the appetite for marvels, the love of the Phony an sich, in itself and for its own sweet sake.'

SYMPLOCE (a)
A figure consisting in the repetition of one word or phrase at the beginning, and of another at the end, of successive clauses or sentences. A combination of anaphora and epistrophe.

CUDDY (b)
A (small) horse. Chiefly dialect and Australian. 1930: 'A stockman apostrophised his bloody cuddy.'

BAWWAYS
a. Forest rides
b. Crookedly
c. Left-handed

SWEEK
a. A trap
b. Weak tea
c. To flog

ANTAPEX
a. A muscle
b. A solar point
c. The toes

AUBUSSON
a. A sausage
b. A tapestry
c. A wild boar

SPISSID
a. Thick
b. Drunk
c. A javelin

BAWWAYS (b)

Crookedly. Leaning awkwardly. Leaning to one side. Sideways. Anglo-Irish. Origin of first element obscure. 1907: 'Scholtz's five crown cloak hung bawways on me.'

SWEEK (a)

Part of a trap for catching birds. Possibly related to 'sweak', to swing. 1623: 'First bait the sweek with a thin piece of good Cheese, or Bacon, or Suet.'

ANTAPEX (b)

The point on the celestial sphere, situated in the constellation Columba, away from which the sun is moving. The point opposite to the apex of the solar way.

AUBUSSON (b)

Tapestry made at Aubusson. Especially a carpet made of this. The toponym of a manufacturing town, department Creuse, France. 1927: 'Wasn't that the dreadful hairy, smelly one [sc. a Russian conspirator] who spoilt your Aubusson?'

SPISSID (a)

Thick. Adaptation of the Latin *spissus*. 1781: 'Around their edges they are environed with a spissid, sub-pellucid liquid, which seems to glue them to the branch.'

BAWLEY
a. A hooligan
b. A game of marbles
c. A boat

BAWNEEN
a. A young woman
b. A weskit
c. The pine marten

SPILUS
a. A spot
b. A quill pen
c. A ball-game

EGERIA
a. A type of china
b. A velocipede
c. A goddess

WOLLY
a. A fool
b. A sheep
c. A policeman

BAWLEY (c)

A fishing-smack peculiar to the coasts of Essex and Kent. Of obscure origin. 1888: 'A little creek where barges and bawley-boats can ride.'

BAWNEEN (b)

In Ireland: a sleeved waistcoat made from undyed flannel worn by farm-labourers. Adaptation of the Irish *báinín*, undyed flannel; *bán*, white.

SPILUS (a)

A spot or mark on the skin. Adaptation of the Greek *spílos*.

EGERIA (c)

In Roman mythology, the name of a goddess, supposed to be the instructress of Numa Pompilius, and regarded as the giver of life. Transferred: a tutelary divinity; a patroness and adviser.

WOLLY (c)

A uniformed police officer, especially a constable. British slang. Origin uncertain, but perhaps connected with 'walloper', 1950s slang for police officer. 1970: 'The wollies were out in their cars, patrolling for drunks and discontents.'

PIPA
a. A toad
b. A female flautist
c. A type of embroidery hem

HUMMEL
a. A haystack
b. Without horns
c. To humiliate

TAMAGOTCHI
a. A toy
b. Grass arrangement
c. A fall at judo

DRABA
a. A loose woman
b. An apron
c. A herb

VIGNERON
a. Twenty
b. A mountain goat
c. A wine grower

PIPA (a)

A genus of South American toads that carry their young on their back. A toad of this genus, the Surinam toad. Surinam dialect.

HUMMEL (b)

Hornless, awnless. Without horns. Scottish variant of 'humble'. As a noun, a hornless stag. A polled or hornless cow. A hummel bonnet – a type of Scotch cap worn by Highland regiments before the introduction of the glengarry (1851). Adaptation of the Low German.

TAMAGOTCHI (a)

A hand-held electronic toy in which an animated pet displayed on a small screen must be kept 'alive' by pushing buttons at regular intervals to simulate feeding, exercise etc. An acquisition from Japanese, where it means literally 'lovable egg'. The craze for the toys reached Britain in 1997. They are also called in the vernacular 'cyberpets'. 1998: 'A French motorist killed a cyclist and injured another when she took her eye off the road trying to save her Tamagotchi virtual pet. The 27-year-old woman became distressed when the electronic pet, which was attached to her key ring, started to send out distress signals.'

DRABA (c)

A plant of the genus of herbs so named belonging to the family *Cruciferae*, found in temperate and arctic regions and cultivated as hardy annual, biennial and perennial alpine plants. Adaptation of the Greek *drabe*, a kind of cress. 1895: 'Latiseptal silicula of Draba.'

VIGNERON (c)

One who cultivates grape-vines. A wine grower. French. 1787: 'I can procure for you the best wines from the vigneron himself.'

AXITE
a. Gunpowder
b. Phoenician letter X
c. Access

COCOBOLO
a. A ball game
b. Mad
c. Timber

VIBRIO
a. A worm
b. A nerve
c. A musical instrument

COBBRA
a. A snake
b. A coffee
c. The head

ELAPID
a. Snakelike
b. Rabbitlike
c. Stony

AXITE (a)
A smokeless powder for sporting rifles, composed of strip cordite in which a little of the gun-cotton is replaced by potassium nitrate. From the -*ax*, in *bonax* and *ptimax*, names of sporting cartridges manufactured by Messrs Kynoch (ICI Metals Ltd).

COCOBOLO (c)
The timber from any one of several species of tree of the Central American genus *Dalbergia*, or the tree itself. Adaptation of the Arawak *kakabali*. 1951: 'Cocobolo, a very hard, dense, tough wood of a bright red colour and variable grain. Familiar through its use in knife handles.'

VIBRIO (a)
A genus of minute nematode worms. An anguillule. Adaptation from the Latin *vibrare*, to vibrate. 1875: 'This has been shown to depend upon the presence of a peculiar vibrio, which lives on the surfaces of wounds and bandages.'

COBBRA (c)
The head, the skull. An Aboriginal word. 1890: 'Having an empty cobbra, as the Blacks would say.'

ELAPID (a)
Of, pertaining to, or resembling a venomous colubrid snake of the family *Elapidae*. 1969: 'The elapid and back-fanged snakes tend to hold onto their prey.'

VOLA
a. A hollow
b. A musical instrument
c. A volition

COCOBAY
a. Long John Silver's harbour
b. A tree
c. Leprosy

BRUTUM FULMEN
a. A bird
b. A threat
c. Mere noise

WEM
a. A pimple
b. To mutilate
c. A safe haven

COWY
a. A seashell
b. Timorous
c. Like a cow

VOLA (a)
The hollow of the hand or foot. Adaptation of the Latin. 1728: 'The Metacarpus, which is the Body of the Hand, including the Dorsum and Vola.'

COCOBAY (c)
A form of leprosy once prevalent in the West Indies. Adaptation of the Twi *kokoba*. 1807: 'The diseases which peculiarly affect them [sc. the Negroes] are the yaws, cocobay, or leprosy, dirt-eating, and the jaw-fall.'

BRUTUM FULMEN (c)
A mere noise. An ineffective act or empty threat. Sound and fury, signifying nothing. Latin for a 'senseless thunderbolt'. 1680: 'It hath been brutum fulmen to us, a thunderbolt of no force.'

WEM (b)
To disfigure, mutilate (a person, his body). To impair (the mind). To injure (a thing). 1500: 'And she after childbearing shall be wemmed of nothing.'

COWY (c)
Of, pertaining to, or characteristic of a cow. Bovine. 1955: 'Freshly drawn milk from an udder has a characteristic flavour, best described as cowy.'

COCUM
a. A yam
b. Lucky
c. A lover

ZERUMBET
a. An aromatic plant
b. A war trumpet
c. A paradox

BRUNE
a. A dark-complexioned girl
b. Fog
c. A Swiss mountaineer's hot toddy

KAKI
a. Poo
b. Persimmon
c. A colour

HIMBO
a. A muscle
b. A pretty thicko
c. A hymn-book

COCUM (b)

Used without precise grammatical reference for that which is (a) advantageous, lucky; (b) proper, correct. Adaptation of the Yiddish *kochem*. 1886: 'The Flippity Flop Young Man, I once was a Member-for-Slocum young man, A know-pretty-well-what-is-cocum young man.'

ZERUMBET (a)

An East Indian plant of the genus *Curcuma*, or its root, used, like the allied Cassumanar and Zenoary, as a tonic drug. Portuguese adaptation of the Hindi and Persian.

BRUNE (a)

A dark-complexioned girl or woman, a brunette. Adaptation of the French. 1865: 'Now with a blonde, and now with a brune.'

KAKI (b)

The Japanese persimmon, or Chinese date-plum. Adaptation of the Japanese name.

HIMBO (b)

An attractive but unintelligent young man; the male equivalent of a bimbo. Originally US. A journalistic coinage of around the time when bimbos were making all the front pages, intended to give equal billing to the mono-braincelled beaux of female film stars and the like.

VEERY
a. Tending to swerve
b. Exceedingly
c. A bird

GREBO
a. A breakfast cereal
b. A punk
c. A fish

TAURYLIC
a. Pertaining to the Minotaur
b. An acid
c. A Trireme sail

HORNERO
a. A bird
b. A longhorn cow
c. An obscene verse

TIRRIT
a. A trumpet
b. A fit
c. A bird

VEERY (c)
The tawny thrush of North America. Probably echoic or imitative.

GREBO (b)
(A member of) an urban youth cult in Britain character-ised by musical tastes bridging heavy metal and punk rock, an aggressive or anti-social manner, and long hair and clothes reminiscent of the earlier biker or greaser generation. Possibly coined from 'greaser' plus the ending '-bo', as in dumbo, jumbo. 1987: 'This is Pop Will Eat Itself's triumphant, Grolsch-soaked finale to a pimply pop pepped twelve-song designer grebo set.'

TAURYLIC (b)
A colourless acid oil, obtained together with phenol from human urine and that of cows and horses.

HORNERO (a)
A South American bird of the genus *Furnarius*, especially *Furnarius rufus*. Also called the baker-bird. 1970: 'The name ovenbirds has often been applied to this family [sc. *Furnariidae*] because of the oven-like nests built by horneros.'

TIRRIT (b)
A fit of fear or temper. An upset, disturbance of one's equanimity. Shakespeare, 2 *Henry IV*, iv, 220: 'Here's a goodly tumult: He forswear keeping house, before I'll be in these tirrits and frights.'

TARSIA
a. Wooden mosaic
b. A Lycian province
c. A card game

KOHEKOHE
a. A dance
b. A fish
c. A tree

TAUTOG
a. A fish
b. Repetition
c. A tax

KHAL
a. A vulture
b. A jungle tribe
c. A creek

TORTOR
a. Chocolate cake
b. A tortoise
c. A torturer

TARSIA (a)
A kind of mosaic inlaid work in wood of various colours and shades. Adaptation of the Italian. 1875: 'The wood veneered or inlaid with marquetry or tarsia work of ivory, ebony, box or palm.'

KOHEKOHE (c)
A deciduous tree, *Dysoxylum spectabile*, which has pinnate leaves and panicles of fragrant white flowers. Maori. 1835: 'Kohekohe – A fine handsome tree, with a trunk free of branches to a height of forty feet.'

TAUTOG (a)
A labroid fish, *Tautoga americana*, also called black-fish or oyster-fish, abundant on the Atlantic coast of North America and esteemed for food. 1888: 'Tautog would consequently seem to be a word from the dialect of the Narragansett Indians.'

KHAL (c)
A creek or river. Bengali. 1958: 'The upper part of the plain between the Garai-Madhumati and the Padma is full of rivers, streams, and khals of various sizes.'

TORTOR (c)
A torturer, tormentor. An executioner. Latin agent noun for *torquere*, *tortum*, to twist. 1610: 'The Tortor proudly did the feat, but clear he went not quit; / That holy Martyr lost his head, this cruel wretch his sight.'

KIMCHI
a. A pickle
b. A male robe
c. A paper game

LADANG
a. Dry land
b. An axe
c. A village court

TETRAPLA
a. Four versions
b. A primitive bra
c. A poem

KHALASI
a. A servant
b. A language
c. An outdoor toilet

HERAT
a. A rodent
b. A carpet
c. Poll tax

KIMCHI (a)
A raw strongly-flavoured vegetable pickle, the Korean national dish. 1925: 'Kimchi, a horrible dish made out of vegetables which have become rotten.'

LADANG (a)
A piece of land under dry cultivation, often a jungle clearing. Malay. 1958: 'Nomads of the deep jungle, they clear and cultivate patches of a few acres, known as ladangs.'

TETRAPLA (a)
A text consisting of four parallel versions, especially that of the Old Testament. Greek for 'fourfold'. 1821: 'They were arranged in four parallel columns, and the work was called Tetrapla.'

KHALASI (a)
A native servant or labourer, especially one employed as a seaman. Hindi. 1957: 'The Lascars, known as khalasies, belong to the Deck Department. They are Moslems.'

HERAT (b)
A rug. The toponym of a city in north-western Afghanistan, used to designate a kind of carpet and rug and the leaf and rosette patterns of such rugs. Also *Herati*.

UMBELLA
a. A parasol
b. Inflorescence
c. A parasitic disease

MORES
a. Second helpings
b. Gumboils
c. Manners

DUB
a. Poetry
b. A learner biker
c. An idiot

KAKAPO
a. A chamber pot
b. The owl-parrot
c. A bain-marie vessel

TUBULAR
a. Terrif
b. Wicked
c. A style of rap

UMBELLA (b)

A mass of inflorescence borne upon pedicels of nearly equal length springing from a common centre. An umbel. Adaptation of the Latin *umbella*, a sun-shade.

MORES (c)

Those acquired customs and social assumptions that give cohesion to a community or social group, the contravention or rejection of which produces a reaction of shock and outrage. Plural of the Latin *mos*, manner, custom.

DUB (a)

A type of Black performance poetry, originally performed extempore and accompanied by dub or other recorded music, but subsequently also written down. 1982: 'I consider Louise Bennett to be the mother of the young dub poets.'

KAKAPO (b)

The New Zealand owl-parrot, large winged but almost flightless. In Maori, *kaka* means parrot, and *po* is night.

TUBULAR (a)

Wonderful, marvellous. A Valspeak (girly slang from San Fernando Valley, Cal) approval adjective taken from US surfers' slang, where it denotes a hollow and curved wave, suitable for riding on. 1982: 'The Zappa's Valley girl becomes, like, a totally tubular national craze – for sure.'

RIC-RAC
a. A braid
b. A gambling game
c. The New Zealand magpie

THAMUDIC
a. Inscriptions
b. Frankincense
c. Magical

DEMIBAR
a. A scholar at New Hall
b. False dice
c. A parry at fencing

TINGLE
a. A skating leap
b. A mollusc
c. A cross-rafter

TEMPS
a. Fishes
b. Ballet movements
c. Flowers

RIC-RAC (a)
Or rick-rack. A decorative braid in open zigzag form, or openwork made with it. Presumably from rack, the instrument of torture?

THAMUDIC (a)
Of, pertaining to, or designating a class of inscriptions in northern and central Arabia dating from the fifth to the first centuries BC, or the ancient Semitic language of which they are the only evidence. 1974: 'Recent archaeological work has revealed numerous Thamudic roick writings and pictures not only on Mt Athlith but also throughout central Arabia.'

DEMIBAR (b)
Name for a kind of false dice. 1592: 'Those are called high Fulloms, low Fulloms. Those Demi-bars, bar Sizeaces.'

TINGLE (b)
Any of several marine molluscs, all of which bore holes in the shells of oysters and other molluscs. Abbreviation of 'whelk-tingle'. 1974: 'The introduction of the American slipper limpet and the American tingle on to the south-east coast of England are well-documented examples.'

TEMPS (b)
A term used in the names of various ballet movements in which there is no transfer of weight from one foot to the other. French literally 'time'. Bernard Shaw, 1890: 'I do not know which particular temps is a battement and which a ronde de jambe.'

DITION
a. Pronunciation
b. Rule
c. A legal protocol

THANX
a. Thank you
b. A fish
c. An edible grass

SNOB
a. A sheep
b. A hat
c. A carpenter's awl

EPIZOON
a. An amoeba
b. A parasite
c. A prehistoric fish

TEMPORALE
a. A musical instruction
b. A turncoat
c. Weather

DITION (b)
Rule. Sway. Jurisdiction. Command. Adaptation of the Latin *diciōn-em*. 1633: 'Under the Roman dition and jurisdiction.'

THANX (a)
Commercial and informal spelling of 'thanks'. Mencken, 1936: 'Such forms as *burlesk thanx* and *kreem* are used freely by the advertising writers.'

SNOB (a)
The last sheep to be sheared. Hence, the roughest or most difficult sheep to shear. Equals a 'cobbler'. Oz and New Zealand slang. 1975: '"Get on to this wrinkled bludger!" he said. It was the last sheep in the pen. "Real snob, ain't it?"'

EPIZOON (b)
A parasitic animal that lives on the exterior of the body of another animal. 1876: 'The Balatro calvus of Claparède, lives as an epizoon.'

TEMPORALE (c)
A weather condition of the Pacific coast of Central America consisting of strong south-west winds bringing heavy rain. Adaptation of the Spanish *temporal*, storm, spell of rainy weather. 1936: 'Twice or more in the season there will be temporales, when it will rain interminably for a week.'

ACKNOWLEDGEMENTS

The Times. Its editors, from Charles Wilson, who introduced 'Lost Words' to an astonished world, and his successors who carry on publishing them. The Literary Society, the *Flaccidae* and *Ad Eundem*. All good wordsmiths, from the Fowler Brothers to William Safire across the pond. Readers, purists, pedants, logophiles and all who love language, and take it seriously, and seize laptops to tap furious letters to newspapers.